THE SERIOUS SEASON

THE SERIOUS SEASON

Daily Lenten Meditations for Everyday Christians

Rev. ROGER A. SWENSON

ALBA · HOUSE　　NEW · YORK

SOCIETY OF ST. PAUL, 2187 VICTORY BLVD., STATEN ISLAND, NEW YORK 10314

Library of Congress Cataloging in Publication Data

Swenson, Roger A.
  The serious season.

  1. Lent — Meditations.   2. Catholic Church — Meditations.
  3. Devotional calendars — Catholic Church.   I. Title.
  BV85.S94   1987   242'.34   86-25876
  ISBN 0-8189-0512-3

Nihil Obstat:
Rev. William F. Maestri
Censor Librorum

Imprimatur:
Most Rev. Philip M. Hannan
Archbishop of New Orleans

Designed, printed and bound in the United States of
America by the Fathers and Brothers of the
SOCIETY OF ST. PAUL, 2187 VICTORY BOULEVARD,
STATEN ISLAND, NEW YORK 10314, *as part of their*
communications apostolate.

---

  2 3 4 5 6 7 8 9 *(Current Printing: first digit)*

© *Copyright 1987 by the Society of St. Paul*

FOREWORD

I am delighted to recommend Father Roger Swenson's new book *The Serious Season*. All of us, and especially lay persons, can be enriched by his thought-provoking meditations for each day throughout Lent. The Church provides us with a very rich fare of Scripture readings and prayers to help us change and grow spiritually. I enjoyed reading the author's reflections and especially his poems at the conclusion of each meditation. These poems are the best part of his book. They have a freshness about them and offer us insights to understand ourselves and our duties more clearly.

As the present chairman of the Bishop's Committee on the Laity in this country, I believe that this new work will be an aid for lay persons to develop their spiritual lives. This book is timely as we look forward to the forthcoming Synod in Rome on the specific mission by the laity in the Church and in the world. Pope John Paul II has expressly asked us to pray for this special intention.

Lay men and women hear God's call to holiness in the very web of their existence. It is in and through the events of the world, the pluralism of modern living, the complex decisions and conflicting values, the richness and fragility of sexual relationships and the delicate balance between activity and stillness that our laity will hear God's call.

Bishops in this country have high hopes that the laity will contribute more and more to the spiritual heritage of the Church. We know their hunger for God's word and their search for spiritual formation and direction in the deep ways of prayer. (See "Called and Gifted: The American Catholic Laity" 1980).

Father Roger Swenson is a busy and dedicated pastor in a large parish in the Archdiocese of New Orleans. I am glad that he took time to share his reflections on the special graces of Lent in a manner that the lay person in the pew can readily understand and appreciate. We all long for a stronger and more enriched faith and *The Serious Season* will help us pray and work toward that goal.

† Most Rev. Stanley Joseph Ott
Bishop of Baton Rouge
Chairman, Bishops' Committee on the Laity

INTRODUCTION

"Father, how long does Lent last?" Few are the Pastors who have not been asked that question. It usually comes up around Passion Sunday triggered by a discussion at the office or the bridge table about plans for an Easter weekend outing or social affair. It's a reasonable question that deserves a reasoned answer. The easiest answer, though not always the most welcome, is chronological: Lent extends from Ash Wednesday to Holy Thursday, and is followed by the three most solemn days of the church's year, the Sacred Triduum.

The reader will find in this book meditations for each of the forty-six days included in the season of Lent and the Triduum. However, the principle underlying these meditations is not chronological. Here, the answer to how long Lent lasts is not "forty-six days," but rather "until you are perfected." Lent is a season in which Christians take serious steps to become perfect.

The idea of perfection is off-putting to many because it seems to imply an impossible goal. Jesus says, "You must be made perfect as your heavenly Father is perfect" (Mt 5:48). But no one can become as perfect as our heavenly Father. Growth toward spiritual wholeness, however, is possible. The early church saw the quest for perfection as a quest for wholeness. The Greek word which modern scholars translate as "perfect" in Matthew's Gospel had a wider, richer connotation for the first Christians who were familiar with the Aramaic original. "Let endurance come to its perfection so that you may be fully mature and lacking in nothing" (Jm 1:4). The *Jerusalem Bible* makes the same point a bit differently, ". . .so that you will become fully developed, complete, with nothing missing." In other words, so that you may become whole, so that you may achieve, in modern terms, a better, healthier integration of the various internal forces, emotions, thought processes, and desires which have so much influence over one's relationship to God.

Purification and penance are recommended to us by the church not to make us hurt but to make us whole. Those areas of our spiritual life which have not reached maturity or which have fallen back into childishness are the non-integrated aspects to which Lenten purification and penance are applied. When Jesus teaches that we must be perfected as our heavenly Father is perfect, he tells us to take time to bring these disparate parts of our spiritual anatomy into equilibrium. Lent is the perfect time for this kind of perfecting.

Purification and penance mean sacrifice, a concept which has never been popular. The very idea of sacrifice repels those who look to a loving God and refuse to believe that he wants us to make ourselves uncomfortable for his sake. They are right to step back from this path to perfection. God's plan is not for us to torture ourselves with meaningless penance and cleansings, nor to give up peripheral pleasures so that our spirit of grumpiness will fit the season. God's plan is for us to become whole. To become well-integrated spiritually requires sacrifice, not holocausts and long faces, but that delicate process which turns a heart of stone into a heart of flesh, the process of perfecting each of one's inner powers and weaknesses so that they achieve that balance called wholeness. The key to this integrating,

Introduction

balancing, perfecting process is the kind of sacrifice known as dedication.

When we dedicate something, we give it over to someone else. In the case of our Lenten sacrifice, we give over to God control of our powers and weaknesses. We ask God to take over for his own use our talent for organization or our weakness for gossip. We ask him to accept and make holy our abundance and our want, to receive and make whole our penchant for flattery or our lack of kindness, to integrate our gift of meditation and our millstone of cowardice. In sum, we ask God to free, by his acceptance, our weaknesses frozen in an immature state and to channel the strengths, which we have used to no good purpose, into his good purposes. This is the dedication, the giving over, which God requires. This is the only sacrifice which pleases him. This is the reason for Lenten purification and penance.

Examining our failings, our lack of integration, is purification, and purification is serious business. Repairing the wrongs caused by our lack of wholeness is penance, and penance is serious business. Thus, the title of this book. It is written to strengthen you in your daily struggle for wholeness. Each of the following pages will help you to be more honest with yourself by suggesting healthy examination of various areas of your life which need purification and require penance. Spend about fifteen minutes with each day's meditation. Most of that time should be given to prayerful consideration of where you have been and where you would like to go in your relationships to God and to his children. The ideas herein are meant to stimulate, not stifle, your meditation. See them as jumping-off points. The daily rhythm of a special, limited time set aside for this kind of prayer will help you examine your spiritual life thoroughly while guarding against introspective tailspins. This process will aid your quest for wholeness by pointing out this inner movement or that lack of growth which needs perfecting. This book takes you and God and your mutual relationship seriously. Each part of you is worthy of dedication to him. Lent is the perfect season for that dedication. May what follows assist you in giving yourself, your *whole* self, to God.

I am grateful to the members of my congregation, the family of St. Anthony of Padua Parish, for the many lessons they have taught me. The dedicated Christian lives of my parishioners have offered me countless insights into the spiritual life, insights which I have employed in these meditations. I am happy to share authorship of this book with these good people.

R. A. S

Daily Lenten Meditations for Everyday Christians

to
my mother and father

ASH WEDNESDAY

Return to me with your whole heart, with fasting, and weeping and mourning. (Jl 2:12)

My boyhood passion was railroads. There were seasons when I spent every waking hour outside of school at the switching yard at the edge of town. I was mesmerized by the intricate gearing of the grimy locomotives, as the tremendous pressures they barely contained forced steam from every groaning valve. Every so often I fell victim to the trainwatcher's occupational hazard — a cinder in the eye. These little bits of ash were not as painful as they were annoying. The only time they made their presence painfully known was when I looked sideways at something.

In this age of renewal, we often look askance at Lent. We view it as an uncomfortable interruption in our progress from life as a vale of tears to life as a celebration of resurrection. Lent becomes a cinder in the eye of our soul, something uncomfortable that enters our vision at the end of every winter. So we quickly look away, straight ahead to the Gospel which seems to support our liberated view. Doesn't Jesus warn us not to look glum, not to flaunt our sacrifices or perform acts for people to see? Isn't this the true Christian transformation of Joel's dour call for fasting, weeping and mourning?

If we believe that Jesus has overturned the ancient admonition to sacrifice, we had better read the Gospel more carefully. True, he warns against outward show, but he does so precisely because it distorts the immutable triad of sacrifice. "When you give alms..., when you are praying..., when you fast...." Jesus takes for granted that his followers know and follow the tradition of sacrifice. What he warns against is the pharisaical thirst for recognition. Lenten sacrifice should be seen only by One. "Then your Father, who sees what no man sees, will repay you" (Mt 6:18).

There are no cinders in God's eye as he looks straight at you and me. "Now is the acceptable time" to shine in the eye of God. We must not let our modern obsession with ease blind us to the fact that we came from ashes and shall end the same way. Immortality will be ours only to the degree that we keep our possible annihilation in plain sight. Ash Wednesday reminds us that we haven't got it made, that even in this age of renewal, it is the striving that counts. Lent is the season for striving, for doing better through sacrifice, for looking death straight in the eye. Only through the purification of prayer, almsgiving, and fasting can we escape the hypnotic gaze of the world and stare down the baleful eye of death.

> It is hard to see the beggar
> with a cinder in your eye.
> So look away lest you go blind.
>
> It is hard to pass the plate by
> when your stomach growls and groans.
> So come, eat well, and fill the void.
>
> It is hard to walk the Stations
> with a stone inside your shoe.
> So sit awhile and ease the pain.
>
> Let the world fill you completely,
> charm your eyes, and heal your wound.
> The world will succor you. For now.

Father in heaven, clear our vision as we begin this season of purification. Help us to see the way your Son set out for us. May his cross made in ashes be the sign of our Lenten sacrifice. Amen.

THURSDAY AFTER ASH WEDNESDAY

Whoever wishes to be my follower must deny his very self, take up his cross each day, and follow in my steps. (Lk 9:23)

Trainers in the art of physical exercise make sure that neophytes don't do too much too soon. "Ease into it," they warn. "Add five minutes to your regimen each day. Don't try to go five miles the first day or you'll pull a muscle."

On this second day of Lent, Jesus gives us his cross. No "ease into it." No slow and steady build-up. Simply, take up your cross. What's the rush, Lord? Can't you see I'm out of shape? My soul has gotten flabby. My conscience has lost its tone. I've got moral muscles that I haven't used in a long time. Too much, too soon and I might not even get out of the starting gate.

Jesus knows well that we Christians can raise procrastination to a high art. He himself had so much to do in so little time. As the second Moses, he had to lead all mankind from slavery to freedom. But the history of his people was against him. Even after Moses had set before the Israelites the choice of life or death, they were slow to choose rightly. Moses did all that he could. "Choose life!" In succeeding generations, prophets repeated the fundamental option. Again and again, the Chosen People recoiled from the blessing and chose the curse.

Since time is running out, you and I must run faster than time. And we must make this dash carrying a burden, a burden called life. Choose life! Take the cross of life upon your shoulders and follow in the footsteps of Jesus. He shouldered life and carried it with him. He bore the sick, the poor, the possessed. All those considered cursed, he transformed into a blessing. Just as people recoiled from the choice Moses offered, so they recoiled from Jesus and his burden.

Choose life! Not the easy life, but life as it is, life made up of the dispossessed and the disinherited. Lent is the time to pick them up and carry them. Lent is today! They hurt today! Do not waste today! If you choose to put off bearing the burden of real life, you have chosen the curse of procrastination. You have let one more day go by without moving life forward. Perhaps you can afford to wait another twenty-four hours, but those crying out in your bleak neighborhoods and your mean streets cannot. Take up your cross, today!

> Lent is newborn, fresh from old ashes.
> For me it starts tomorrow.
>
> The poor are age-old and always with us.
> I'll tend to them tomorrow.
>
> Sin is timeless, as old as Adam.
> Lord, wash me clean tomorrow.
>
> Life seems endless, so slow to wear out.
> I'll be reborn tomorrow.

Eternal Father, look upon us locked in time and teach us the value of today. Make us bold to seize this day and guide us on your path during this Holy Season.   Amen.

FRIDAY AFTER ASH WEDNESDAY

> This, rather, is the fasting that I wish:
> releasing those bound unjustly,
> untying the thongs of the yoke;
> Setting free the oppressed,
> breaking every yoke;
> Sharing your bread with the hungry,
> sheltering the oppressed and the homeless;
> Clothing the naked when you see them,
> and not turning your back on your own. (Is 58:6-7)

During the summers of my college days, I lived and worked in a settlement house among the poorest of the poor. It was my first experience of prolonged self-giving. Day after day, my co-workers and I gave all of our time and energy to needy children. Yet despite the joy I felt, joy which even now I cannot describe, I always sensed a barrier between my children and me. They never opened themselves completely to me as I thought I did to them.

One day, in a quiet, open moment, I asked a teenager about his aura of reserve. Why did he and the others always seem to hold back their deepest feelings? "Because," he said, "in August you will leave and we will still be here."

Fasting is not a method of gaining merit in God's eyes. He already loves us with an infinite love. Fasting is a way of being poor. We choose to enter poverty and live for a time with those who have no choice. Yet we have an out. Our fast will come to an end, an end we usually anticipate with relief.

An authentic fast must be a life project. By condemning our stomachs to poverty during Lent, we sentence ourselves to a term of duress, an imprisonment of hopelessness which simulates the despair of those who have no choice. But the sentence of the poor is not reduced by good behavior. If we seek true solidarity with them, our voluntary fast must be a symbol of our determination to live poor always. That's quite a daunting phrase — "to live poor always." It means to live from hand to mouth, to rely on others for everything. When that "Other" is God, we become the "poor in spirit" blessed by Jesus.

On the Fridays of Lent, we are urged to become poor in spirit, to make ourselves feel the pain of hunger, and in so doing, to feel the poor man's dependence on others. Perhaps our groaning bellies will prod us to seek a solution to the problem of the poor around us. Pain wonderfully concentrates one's attention.

If we do find an answer which we can apply to the poor of our neighborhood, the poor of the world will still be here tomorrow. We can stand with all of them only if our bodily fasting is a symbol of our spiritual detachment, of our willingness to rely on God alone and to reject, at the cost of our ease, what is not from Him.

> The poor always surround us.
> They stand in our light
>   and make us blink our eyes.
>
> But they never attack us
> or march rank on rank
>   up to our window panes.
>
> The poor know their low station,
> the place we assign.
>   They shrink from our mad pace.
>
> Yet Christ, ever among them,
> today and the next,
>   remains when we will not.

Father of the poor, may this Lenten fast strengthen our kinship with those who have only you to rely on. Let us learn the meaning of true poverty of spirit as we reach out to relieve the sufferings of your little ones. Amen.

SATURDAY AFTER ASH WEDNESDAY

> The healthy do not need a doctor; sick people do. I do not come to invite the self-righteous to a change of heart, but sinners. (Lk 5:31-32)

Part of every Christian's ministry is to visit the sick. As a priest, I have occasion to bring Holy Communion to the homebound. I make it a point before ministering the Eucharist to ask if the parishioner wants to go to Confession. Frequently, an octogenarian's answer makes me chuckle inside. He or she will say, "What sins would I have? I can't even get out of the house."

Often, you and I rest easily in a similar assumption. We are not world travelers or public persons. Our lives are circumscribed by duties to our families, obligations as employees and citizens, and a rare foray into the world of entertainment or recreation. When Lent rolls around and we hear the call to repentance, we think, "What sins could I have? My daily trek from home to work to the supermarket to the bank or post office and back home doesn't leave much room for sinning."

Lent could be called the "Serious Season." It is a time for even the best of us to get serious about the offense we give to God and neighbor. Any thought, no matter how fleeting, which offends God, has cosmic proportions. Any act, no matter how unreflective, which injures others, harms the whole world. Of course, scrupulosity is to be avoided, but if the fabric of justice is torn, in the words of Willy Loman, "attention must be paid."

Seemingly trifling acts of rudeness, thoughtlessness, gossiping, rash judgment, or bad example throw a monkey wrench into God's plan for justice. The chaotic state of today's world has its origin much more in millions of trifling sins than in single acts of terrorism or barbarity. Pope Paul VI told us that if we want peace, we must work for justice. The peaceful world we all seek is but a glimmering hope when justice flickers out in the hearts of millions of Christians.

In this Serious Season, we measure our thoughts, words and actions against God's plan for justice as found in the Ten Commandments, the Beatitudes, and the other teachings of Christ and of his Church. Christ came to call not the self-righteous, but sinners. And that means all of us. "If we say, 'we have never sinned,' we make Him a liar" (1 Jn 1:10). His call goes unanswered in self-righteous hearts. Each of us is an important part of the peaceful kingdom for which we pray. A healthy and comprehensive examination of our past based on God's plan for justice is proof that we take this season seriously.

>I heard a muffled call last night.
> It echoed within me
> but came from outside me.
>   I did not reply.
>
>I would have answered, "Here I am,"
> had it been my number.
> It was for a sinner.
>   He did not reply.

The Lord was counting One to Ten.
"Injustice" was the word
that broke through my conscience.
I did not reply.

The words came clear then. I had sinned.
"No, Jesus, not guilty!
Please bless my perfection."
He did not reply.

Merciful Lord, help us admit our failings. Though our sins be mere pebbles, they send ripples across the peaceful sea. Since we are too eager to absolve ourselves of injustice, give us the courage to see our lives as you see them.   Amen.

FIRST SUNDAY OF LENT

The devil then took him up a very high mountain and displayed before him all the kingdoms of the world in their magnificence, promising, "All these will I bestow on you if you prostrate yourself in homage before me." At this, Jesus said to him, "Away with you, Satan!" (Mt 4:8-10)

Between the temptations of Jesus in the desert and the night in the Garden of Gethsemane when he asked that the cup of suffering might pass from him stretched many months, perhaps as much as three years. We can be sure that the temptations depicted in today's Gospel are examples — powerful and fearsome, to be sure — of the kinds of trials Jesus endured during his public ministry and, no doubt, during his whole life. Yet, while agreeing to this, most of us would prefer to think of the temptations of the Son of God as somehow different from the mundane urgings to evil with which we must struggle. We like to see Jesus as a figure of might, a divine hero locked in cosmic contention with Satan, battling over "all the kingdoms of the world in their magnificence."

Unfortunately, this kind of selective meditation on the life of the Lord lends itself to a distorted picture of our relationship to our Savior. The result is a chasm between our experience of life and his. We make Jesus a marble statue on a mountain, a Christ of the Andes saving us with a sweep of his mighty hand. Cold and aloof, this Jesus is drained of all humanity. In this flawed assessment of his mission, we are the losers for we have nothing in common with him, no mutual experience of life to nourish us when we suffer reverses in the everyday struggle against our personal temptations.

Those who subscribe to the theory of Jesus-as-Wizard-of-Oz should take a refreshing dip into the waters of the Letter to the Hebrews: "For we do not have a high priest who is unable to sympathize with our weakness, but one who was tempted in every way that we are, yet never sinned" (Heb 4:15).

"Tempted in every way that we are" is mighty inclusive. Could it mean that Jesus, observing the fine living made by a careful rabbi, felt the same twinge of envy we experience at the sight of a fellow worker's new house? Could it mean that Jesus, sitting among the revelers at a country feast, was attacked by the same powerful thirst for more than enough wine as we are at the end of a draining day's work? Had Jesus, looking upon an amply proportioned daughter of Moses, to deal with the same flash of desire which sears the imagination of a red-blooded American male sitting at poolside?

If, as our faith demands, we believe that Jesus was fully

man as well as fully God, the conclusion is compelling. The temptations in the desert and in the Garden are telling examples of countless trials, great and small, that lay between these mileposts. Jesus did not leave the desert and retire to a pedestal on a mountain to return to real life only on the day before he died. He lived every day right here in our world and fought the secret battles that we must fight against our inner urgings.

With one important difference: He won every battle. He "was tempted in every way that we are, yet never sinned." We lose, not every struggle, but enough to disturb us, enough to make us come close to giving up on occasion. We cannot take these losses lightly. Lent reminds us that temptations, though not sinful in themselves, are to be taken seriously. Temptation is the antechamber of sin, that place where we have the last chance to say "Yes" or "No" to evil. Jesus himself entered that antechamber as often as we do. He always turned on his heel and walked out. Too often, we don't even break our stride.

Today, consider your temptations. You know them very well. You know that you will enter the antechamber again and again. You also know that One among all men and women always walked away. Turn to him, now, before evil beckons anew. Ask him to be with you in time of temptation. He has been there before. He knows the way out.

> Temptation is the herald
> announcing pleasure near,
> a muted trumpet crooning:
> There's nothing much to fear.
>
> The cost is very little,
> an hour or two of rue
> in trade for what is wanting.
> It's really just your due.

Some say Christ lacks the knowledge
of struggles such as these.
His battle is with Satan
not these slight reveries.

But His way was the pattern
for every Christian life,
a spectrum wide comprising
great storms and minor strife.

He turned His back on Satan's
grand plans and little lures.
So trust Him when the option
for good or ill is yours.

Lord Jesus, strong to save, quick to pardon, strengthen me in temptation's hour. Your name on my lips will call me back from the brink. Give me the courage to say "Yes" to you and "No" to evil. Amen.

MONDAY OF THE FIRST WEEK

The king will answer them: "I assure you, as often as you did it for one of my least brothers, you did it for me." (Mt 25:40)

One of the most impressive phenomena of our age is the widespread quest for spiritual wholeness. This thirst is by no means limited to Christians or even to those who believe in God. Systems of spiritual health range from Transactional Analysis to est to yoga. Whether they be secular or religious, these methods all have the same touchstone — the ability to center one's self. There is a great deal to be said for centering prayers and mantras and similar techniques. The danger arises when practitioners begin to center themselves *on* themselves.

The insight of Jesus in this regard is not to be overlooked. He knew that, when we heard his words about the king who consigned his subjects to eternal punishment or eternal life, we would first center our thoughts on ourselves. What would be more natural than to seek first personal salvation? He knew also that we would have a tendency to stick with that thought, to plan and polish our lives as perfectly as possible so as to be numbered with the sheep rather than with the goats on the day of judgment. True to form, we do spend the majority of our time looking out for Number One. And so Lent is often observed as the season for getting our own house in order.

This housecleaning must have a wider purpose. There are no solo flights to heaven. We are saved as a community or we are not saved at all. The very specific Biblical emphasis on a covenant people, the shepherd and his flock, the community of believers, finds its modern counterpart in the often-repeated phrase of the Fathers of the Second Vatican Council: the People of God.

Today's passage from the Gospel of Matthew provides a healthy and quite pointed balance to the fallacy of self-centered salvation. In his story of the just king, Jesus outlines precisely how the People of God should approach the question of eternal life. They are to save the hungry by feeding them, rescue strangers by welcoming them, free the imprisoned by visiting them. If there is a nursing home in your neighborhood, or a shelter for the homeless, a food bank, a hospital, or a jail, then you have the opportunity to counter egocentric salvation. Make Lent a time for penance with a purpose. Gather with the People of God.

I dreamed I went to heaven one night
and stood before the throne.
The Mighty One looked down on me.
He looked at me, alone.

"Where are your friends?" I heard Him say.
I offered this reply,
"They're coming right behind, I think.
They'll be here by and by."

I thought of all the nameless ones
still waiting for my love,
the old, the sick, the hungry flock,
while I stood here above.

They'll be here someday, I am sure.
They'll mount to heaven's gate.
"Until that day," the Shepherd said,
"you'll have to stand and wait."

Heavenly Father, make me weak, not strong. Let me know how heavy are the burdens my brothers and sisters must bear so that I might give my strength to them. Show me the needy of your flock and I will gather with them.   Amen.

TUESDAY OF THE FIRST WEEK

Forgive us the wrong we have done as we forgive those who wrong us. (Mt 6:12)

What a difference two little letters can make! I was in an airport recently, rushing from one plane to another, when I stepped into a restroom. All airports seem to be under constant renovation. In this one, the upper walls of the passageways were being painted; a painter's dropcloth partially obscured the sign above the restroom door. It wasn't until I became the object of several startled female stares that I realized the cloth had covered just two little letters on the sign, "w" and "o." I quickly decided I would rest elsewhere.

Two little letters make a big difference in the version of the Lord's Prayer we find in Matthew's Gospel. Just an "a" and an "s," but that seemingly insignificant "as" which they form introduces a promise which is hard to keep. "Forgive me, Lord, *in the same way* I forgive others."

Lent is a time for making promises. Often they are soon broken because they were too grandiose. We promise God to change our lives, mend our ways, give up long-standing habits, fast rigorously, pray always, tithe. We usually bite off more than we can chew and end up feeling guilty about our weakness.

A more reasonable approach would be to concentrate on the little things, things as small as that "as" in the Lord's Prayer. There is not much we can do about past failures to forgive, except learn from them. But we can promise God to do better the next time someone injures us. I refer here not so much to those situations in which someone asks our forgiveness. That is a "best case" scenario. It is a sad fact that most people do not ask us to pardon them. When they do, however, it is relatively easy to forgive.

More often, we receive the hurt but not the request for forgiveness. This is when that little "as" takes on formidable proportions. To forgive without being asked, to forgive silently and compassionately in our hearts, is to forgive as Jesus did. Most of those who received his forgiveness in the Gospels never asked for it, including those who stood jeering beneath his cross.

We ourselves rely on God's constant mercy to fall upon us even when we don't ask for it. It is not easy for us to forgive others with the same constancy. But it is possible to make the promise. This holy season is the right time to ask for Jesus' help in forming the habit of constant mercy.

As we forgive those who trespass against us:	seventy times seven, absolving all my sins.
Can I ask my Lord for constant forgiveness	Constant His mercy and endless my heart's need:
when those who hurt me are lacking my pardon?	Let me forgive them who don't know they hurt me.
I can, for I know that Jesus forgives me	Let me forgive them for Jesus forgives me.

Compassionate Father, as you sent your Son to be mercy-made-flesh in our midst, so now grant me a forgiving heart. Let me pardon as Jesus pardoned, even those who do not seek my absolution. Amen.

WEDNESDAY OF THE FIRST WEEK

Jonah began his journey through the city, and had gone but a single day's walk announcing, "Forty days more and Nineveh shall be destroyed," when the people of Nineveh believed God; they proclaimed a fast and all of them, great and small, put on sackcloth. (Jon 3:4-5)

"Alright, class," Miss Tirant announced, "close your books for a snap quiz." Those last two words have brought terror to the hearts of students ever since teachers and young people were first joined in their uneasy alliance. Since Lent is a school for sacrifice, it is time for you to take a snap quiz: Now, without peeking, what is the difference between the Biblical character known as Jonah and all the other Old Testament prophets?

Not his reluctance to be sent: It required a big fish to get Jonah to where God wanted him, but it also took a lot of divine cajoling to get the likes of Jeremiah and Isaiah and Ezekiel to accept their ministries. Not his message: It was as stark as the proclamation of other prophets: "Repent! Change your ways! Obey God's law, not man's!"

The difference between Jonah and most of his fellow prophets was that Jonah was *successful*. And what a success! In just one day, he turned Nineveh around. Even the cattle had to fast. Almost all of the other Old Testament prophets met with anything but success. Many were rejected. Not a few were killed for their efforts.

At Baptism, each of us was anointed as a prophet. Lent is an opportune time to recall our prophetic charism and speak out for the Lord. There are many places in our communities where the presence of Christ needs to be made manifest. When you pass the pornographic book rack at the checkout counter, ask to see the manager and make him feel the Lord's presence. When your children bring home those depraved tapes and records, make them know the Lord's presence. When God is blasphemed in the language of the workplace, counter this affront with the authentic words of

Christ. To prophesy means to profess your faith in word and action.

But remember, Jonah's success was not typical. Like most prophets, you may be derided or ignored. Your words of truth may even cause a loss of favor with your friends. The history of prophecy has few Jonahs and many Jeremiahs and John the Baptists. God will be with you as he was with them, for you are doing his work. Lent is not only a season for purification. It is also a time to pour the healing balm of God's truth on our world and renew the face of the earth.

> To me, words are precious
> each one a fragile thread.
> And so I gather them
> > polish them
> > husband them
> > measure them
> > ration them.
>
> But I cannot stretch them
> to fit your message, Lord.
> I cannot shout them
> > arm them
> > flaunt them
> > strew them
> > preach them.
>
> Enflesh my thin words, Lord,
> that men will understand
> your wish to convince them
> > console them
> > embrace them
> > forgive them
> > redeem them.

Lord of all Truth, let your Word take flesh in my life. Make me great-souled, big enough to be a fit dwelling for your Truth. Embolden me that I may fearlessly proclaim your message in my world. Amen.

THURSDAY OF THE FIRST WEEK

Treat others the way you would have them treat you: this sums up the law and the prophets. (Mt 7:12)

In Judaic literature, there is an ancient story about a Rabbi named Hillel. Hillel was known not only for his wisdom, but also for his wit. In an attempt to trip him up, one of his students asked Hillel to explain the whole Law while the student stood on one foot. As the student raised his foot, Hillel answered, "That which displeases you do not do to another. This is the whole Law; the rest is commentary."

Whether the Golden Rule is couched in negatives as Hillel did or more positively as it comes from the lips of Jesus in Matthew's Gospel, it must be taken seriously in this Serious Season. We should take time to remember how we may have distorted the Golden Rule to our own ends. Sometimes we cast it in terms of oneupmanship: "Do unto others *before* they do unto you." Sometimes we use it as a bargaining chip: "Do unto others *so that* they will do unto you." Either way, we end up the loser.

Many of us are masters at the "pre-emptive strike," unleashing our arsenals of put-downs and caustic jabs before the other person can do the same to us. We fear their attack because we know how vulnerable we are. We are weak and ridiculous at times, so we are quick to point out the same foibles in others, doing it to them before they can do it to us.

At other times, we invest in our own self-esteem by paying fulsome compliments and expecting to be flattered in return. We are so unsure of our own worth that we would even shout compliments into an echo chamber. That's what the person who is the ostensible object of our praise becomes — a human echo chamber.

Lent shines the bright light of truth on these distortions of the Golden Rule. This is the season to be vulnerable and humble, to admit that we have needs which neither we nor the world can fulfill. Purification and penance imply a lack of wholeness. If we spend these forty days living with the illusion that we are fully self-integrated human beings, we remain untouched by Christ's call to reform our lives.

To "treat others the way you would have them treat you" is not to seek the upper hand over anyone or to flatter in the hope of a like return. Rather, the degree to which we keep the Golden Rule is a measure of our recognition of the right of each of our neighbors to be treated honestly and with dignity.

> If I, limping, steady you,
> our step is surer.
>
> If I, weeping, comfort you,
> our loss decreases.
>
> If I, failing, strengthen you,
> our weakness conquers.
>
> If I, dying, rescue you,
> our life has meaning.

Father of all humanity, you asked your Son to do for us what we would not do for each other. Help us to see in his sacrifice the dignity which you have given to each of our brothers and sisters. May we honor and serve them as Jesus honored and served us.   Amen.

FRIDAY OF THE FIRST WEEK

If you bring your gift to the altar and there recall that your brother has anything against you, leave your gift at the altar, go first to be reconciled with your brother, and then come and offer your gift. (Mt 5:23-24)

The liturgists of Jesus' day, the scribes and the Pharisees, put ritual before anything else. There was only one guide to proper public worship and that was the way of the Law — the Law as interpreted by the scribes and the Pharisees. The rules for the public performance of worship were absolute. Woe be to him who changed a jot or a tittle. Gehenna was too good for the man who absented himself from the solemnities of the Sabbath.

In his conflicts with the scribes and the Pharisees, Jesus often stepped on their legalistic toes when it came to Sabbath observance. He cured on the Sabbath. He allowed his disciples to pick grain for their own daily need on the Sabbath. In today's Gospel, he goes so far as to advocate interruption of the sacred ritual for something more important. "Leave your gift at the altar," he says. "Go first to be reconciled with your brother." Healing a broken relationship is more important than ritualistic perfection.

Do your Lenten resolutions include reconciliation? Perhaps you have chosen to fast, to aid the poor, to visit the Blessed Sacrament, to attend a weekday Mass, but what about that longstanding quarrel which time has not erased? Certainly, you could get along quite well with this coldness between you and your former friend. The earth has kept spinning these many months; you have survived. Anyway, you have forgiven her in your heart and that's what is important. Look at all the other things you are doing for Lent. They are important.

Jesus agrees. Every good thing you are doing is important. He considered proper, heartfelt worship of his Father essential. But one thing outranked them all — reconciliation. Repairing the torn threads of a relationship should interrupt even the ritual of worship. "Go first to be reconciled" else your gift at the altar is unacceptable.

Just as sisters and brothers make up the assembly around the altar of sacrifice at Mass, so this season of sacrifice is a fabric of family relationships and friendships. When pride or selfishness break a thread in this fabric, Lent begins to sag, to lose its spiritual resilience. Our most important work, our first duty is to repair this broken skein of human relationships. Reconciliation renews the fabric of faith which holds God's people together.

It happened. It's over. I can't do much about it.	The altar is waiting for gifts which are untarnished.
She hurt me. I'm human. Let time produce its healing.	The Savior is calling for reconciliation.
I'll worship. I'll promise to fast, to pray and then some.	His people are longing to bind up wounds which fester.
But not that, not pardon. That sacrifice means weakness.	My weakness cries out for Christ's power of forgiveness.

Father of the human family, accept my sorrow for my lack of forgiveness. Transform the weakness which lets pride rule my life. Melt my hardened heart and make me an Apostle of reconciliation. Amen.

SATURDAY OF THE FIRST WEEK

In a word, you must be made perfect as your heavenly Father is perfect. (Mt 5:48)

When Jesus tells us that we must become perfect, he is testing us by fire. This fire is the struggle to love our enemies. Love of our friends is natural; love of those who are repugnant to us is nothing short of a supernatural act of will. Thinking of those who give us pain tends to focus our attention on the pain itself; we get stuck there and are seldom able to proceed to the good that God has surely placed in each of those who oppose us.

In the face of this seemingly impossible task, it is wiser to begin closer to home. Our word "perfect" is a rather inexact translation of the Greek word for "whole." As the author of the Gospel saw it, Jesus was telling his followers that they had to be made whole as their heavenly Father was whole. To be whole means to have all the parts you need and to have them integrated with one another. Perhaps it is so hard to love others because we don't love certain parts of ourselves.

During Lent, we should strive for personal wholeness. Most of us are far from complete self-integration. We are like the dog, Snoopy, in the Peanuts comic strip who often walks around with his feet complaining and his stomach arguing with his head. Not every one of our spiritual or emotional parts has matured at the same rate. This lack of integration is seen in childish spates of anger or envy, and immature overindulgence or egocentricity.

The rain falls on the good and the bad in us. We are what we are at this moment, warts and all. We strive to become more fully human, more whole as our Father is whole. Sometimes we succeed; sometimes we fail. The important thing is to love ourselves, our strengths and weaknesses, *today*. For God loves us *today*. Loving our strengths and our weaknesses, he loves us.

Don't let the word "perfection" frighten you. If you are trying to do God's will, you are closer to wholeness now than you were a year ago or five years ago. Don't let the parts of you that are still weak discourage you. Lent is a time for self-acceptance as much as it is a time for self-accusation. Spend a moment asking God how much he loves you. He will constantly direct your attention to the cross. That's how much he loves you, every part of you. It takes time, but once convinced of God's love for everything that adds up to you, you will find it easier to love others as God loves them, warts and all.

> Monet
> dropped a thousand dots
> on a yard of muslin.
> Bathers splash you.
> A boater tips his hat.
> The Seine sparkles in sunlight.
> If you look very closely
> at the dots,
> you'll see
> dots.
>
> Saint-Saens
> left a thousand notes
> on a ream of paper.
> Cuckoos mock you.
> A jackass brays and snorts.
> The woods rustle in windsong.
> Listen now very closely
> to the notes:
> You hear
> notes.

Rodin
cut a thousand flaws
into pristine marble.
Man sits thinking.
He ponders, plans, and prays.
His soul darkens, then brightens.
If you look very closely
at the flaws,
you'll see
flaws.

Father, my Creator and Sustainer, you have wondrously formed me and know my every longing. Your love is my life. Let me love the life you have given me. Amen.

SECOND SUNDAY OF LENT

Jesus took Peter, James and his brother John and led them up a high mountain by themselves. He was transfigured before their eyes. His face became as dazzling as the sun, his clothes as radiant as light. (Mt 17:1-2)

I must have missed something in my childhood. I cannot recall ever picturing God, the Father, as an old man with a long white beard. This notion of the divinity, so common among small children throughout the ages, never entered my imagination. Perhaps it was Sister Mary Michael's fault. In her no-nonsense way, she made it very clear that God cannot be seen because he is a spirit and spirits don't have faces. I took her at her word. Who was I to disregard the voice of the Church and spend my idle moments dreaming of a face that wasn't there?

Sister said that if you want to know what God looks like, look at a picture of the Sacred Heart. This was good advice, making it a lot easier than conjuring up a portrait of a pure spirit. But as I grew older, the familiar face of the Sacred Heart lost its appeal. It was too . . . well, too nice. That winsome smile, those perfect, somehow feminine features were nothing like the mugs of anyone I knew. The closest match was the face of Errol Flynn, and I was given to believe that he was rather naughty, not to be mentioned in the same breath with the Sacred Heart. So besides being incapable of imagining the features of God, the Father, I had no face for Jesus either.

Then I discovered the Shroud of Turin. The face of that crucified man was a common face. It became more common in the 1960's with the advent of long hair and beards for young men. The face on the Shroud could be seen in factories, farm fields, protest marches, even in my own mirror. I have never been absolutely convinced that the Shroud held Jesus of Nazareth, but it gives me a feeling for the look of his contemporaries. His appearance must have been unremarkable, his face like that of many others of his day. Why else would Judas have to make an identifying kiss part of his dirty deal with the authorities?

On the mountain of the Transfiguration, that unremarkable Galilean face changed. The Gospel gives us little help in the description department. His face was "dazzling as the sun," "transfigured," "changed in appearance." We do know that Peter, James, and John were frightened nearly to death by the radiant clothes, the Old Testament specters, the voice from the cloud. But I think what scared them most was the change in the Master's features. His wasn't just another common face anymore. They weren't sure who he was, but he wasn't the comfortable, approachable Jesus.

The glory that transfigured Jesus was God giving

mankind a test. Was the world ready to accept the power of divinity walking the earth? No, mankind — at least that portion represented by Peter, James, and John — was not ready, nor will we ever be ready in this life to contemplate the unveiled nature of God. We must put a face on it, a common face, our face. The Father made Jesus his human face so that you and I wouldn't be falling into ecstasies every time we saw a selfless mother, a generous benefactor, a homeless family seeking shelter. Whenever someone in need confronts us, whenever a witness to the Gospel gives the gift of self, there is the human face of God masking divine power, a power we must always seek but which we are incapable of assimilating in this dispensation.

As you meditate on the mystery of the Transfiguration, think of those people in whom you experience the power of God. Picture their faces — unremarkable, irregular, everyday mugs masking divinity. If you want to know what Jesus looked like, look at them.

> Picasso's shattered looking glass
> reflects a face in shambles,
> a crazy quilt of eyes and ears
> that never were or will be.
>
> Yet He who painted Pablo's face
> could look at Humpty Dumpty
> and in the fractured features see
> what was and what can still be.
>
> If you would know the face of Christ,
> seek not divine perfection,
> but gaze with God on broken men
> who are and always will be.

My Father, I accept the fact that you could have made me perfect, but chose not to. Help me to see in my imperfections golden opportunities to receive your healing grace and to be compassionate to my broken brothers and sisters. Amen.

MONDAY OF THE SECOND WEEK

Remember not against us the iniquities of the past; may your compassion quickly come to us, for we are brought very low. (Ps 79:8)

To meditate on the being of God is to be struck by his otherness. He is completely different from us. Every attribute of his surpasses ours to an infinite degree. We ration our love; he is all loving. We struggle to learn; his knowledge is infinite. Our puny labors exhaust us: his power created the world. Yet there is one human faculty which seems to put God in the shade: memory. Our memory must be stronger than God's because we are constantly asking him to forget our sins while we cling tenaciously to our grievances against others.

"Remember not against us the iniquities of the past," begs the Psalmist. Do not only forgive our sins, Lord, but forget them. We rely on God not to hold a grudge against us at the same time as we throw fresh salt into the wounds we have carried within us for months and years. Why do we nurse these grudges? It may be we need them to prove that we are worthy of better treatment at the hands of our neighbors. It may be that we don't want to give our tormentor the peace that comes with being forgiven. Most often, we hold grudges out of a perverted sense of justice:

Monday of the Second Week

The only way to balance the scales is to let the scoundrel feel our animosity, to let him or her know the loss of our friendship. In any case, the grudges which make us feel so noble cause our world to grow colder.

Last Saturday in Matthew's Gospel, Jesus told us that we must be perfected as our Father is perfect, that we must be made whole as our Father is whole. Today in Luke's Gospel, he says, "Be compassionate as your Father is compassionate." Compassion must have a great deal to do with wholeness. You can't withhold compassion, you can't nurse a grudge, and expect to be made whole.

"Compassion" means "to suffer *with*." The grudge-holder is not willing to walk a mile in the other person's moccasins, not willing to see the forces which press upon the other and caused him or her to strike at us. But, oh, how quickly we turn to God and ask him to recognize the headache, the cold breakfast, the flat tire, the argument with our spouse which triggered those harsh words toward our workmate. Forget my offense, Lord, for you know the pressures upon me.

Shouldn't we strive for the same loss of memory when someone injures us? I read about an amnesiac who suddenly regained his memory after fourteen years. He found himself in a strange town, with a family he didn't know, unable to find his way to work. A very sad story, indeed. But he also woke up with no grudges, no hates, no desire to repay any injuries. What a blessing in disguise! You and I should cultivate a kind of selective amnesia when it comes to those who sin against us. And pray in confidence to a forgetful God.

In God's wide eye
there is no time.
He is not chained
to yesterdays.

His now is
today and
tomorrow.

No memory
of past offense
can pinch His smile.
In His wide eye

our sin meets
our shame in
this moment.

While we enjoy
the luxury
of pardon held
and wounds unsalved,

so noble,
but never
forgetting,

He bides our time
in patient grace.
A decade or
a century

mean nothing
when Love is
the Watchman.

All-seeing Father,. You sent your Son to teach us to forgive. Now, teach us to forget. Heal our memories. Bind up the old wounds which keep us from compassion.   Amen.

TUESDAY OF THE SECOND WEEK

The scribes and the Pharisees have succeeded Moses as teachers; therefore, do everything and observe everything they tell you. But do not follow their example. Their words are bold but their deeds are few. (Mt 23:2-3)

I have two fine nephews, strapping teenagers who know how to have fun and how to eat. They came to visit me one summer and attended my morning Mass at which I preached a short homily on preserving our environment.

Tuesday of the Second Week

We went to a fair in the city in the afternoon. As we got out of the car in the vast parking lot, I emptied a few matches from the ashtray onto the pavement. I am concerned about public cleanliness and I can't remember ever doing something like that before. I silently rail at people in cars ahead of me who throw beer cans out of their windows. I could argue that I was worried about a fire in the car, but I kept quiet, and so did the boys. My hypocrisy spoke for itself.

No one is immune from hypocrisy. It is one of those "little" sins that have far-reaching effects. Parents, teachers, religious, everyone whose good example is pivotal in forming young consciences has wrestled with "do as I say, not as I do." Jesus singled out the scribes and the Pharisees for their everyday hypocrisy precisely because their everyday responsibility was moral education.

Every Christian, whether he or she likes it or not, is a religion teacher. Even our most interior attitudes are somehow revealed in our actions. During Lent, we should take time to measure our actions against our words. If I fulminate against the immorality of much that is called entertainment on television, and then shoo the kids away from the set while I watch an R-rated movie, what does that say to them? That when they're older, they can watch junk like I do? If I am a coach who extols the virtues of a healthy regimen while my players know I am going to bloat myself on beer at a post-game party, what does that say to them? That they'll have to wait until they're older to ruin their health?

Am I any better than those in today's Gospel who "bind up heavy loads, hard to carry, to lay on other men's shoulders, while they themselves will not lift a finger to budge them" (Mt 23:4)?

Jesus reminds us that hypocrisy cuts both ways. Besides dimming the light of idealism in the eyes of the beholder, we also risk the judgment that *"all* their works are performed to be seen" (Mt 23:5), so that even the good we do becomes suspect. In this Serious Season, take seriously your role as teacher. Whether your classroom is the home, the office, or the church, practice the only scholastic discipline which merits a Ph.D. in Christianity: good example.

>Who dares to teach
>risks all in each
>encounter with
>a choice.
>
>The words that went
>before get bent.
>The deed distorts
>the voice.
>
>Should you then cease
>to speak of peace
>because your heart
>hides wrath?
>
>Or gently lead
>both word and deed
>along the Lord's
>true path.

Father of Truth, Source of all good, we fail so often to match our deeds to our words. Give us the wisdom to know your will and the courage to carry it out. Make us Master Teachers in the school of Christian example. Amen.

WEDNESDAY OF THE SECOND WEEK

> The mother of Zebedee's sons came up to him accompanied by her sons, to do him homage and ask him a favor. "What is it you want?" he said. She answered, "Promise me that these sons of mine will sit, one at your right hand and the other at your left, in your kingdom." In reply Jesus said, "You do not know what you are asking. Can you drink of the cup I am to drink of?" "We can," they said. (Mt 20:20-22)

"Be careful what you wish for; you may get it." Various forms of this old saw have been around for a long time. James and John and their mother probably knew of it. Yet their eyes were so full of what they thought Jesus to be that they had no hesitation in pledging to drink of the cup which Jesus was to drink. To them, the cup was filled with a glorious brew of victory and honor. They wanted to sit beside the King when he came into his own. They would be his counselors, noblemen in the court of the Messiah.

Had James and John been deaf to Jesus' prediction of His passion which immediately precedes this passage? In a sense, yes. They seemed to suffer from a self-inflicted deafness which muted all but what they wanted to hear. All they wanted to hear was the part about the glory.

Lent should be a season of quiet moments when we can concentrate on what the Lord is saying to us, a time to listen to the whole message and not just to what we want to hear. These quiet moments can help us to pray better, for they allow us the time we need to compare our wishes and desires with God's plan.

Are your prayers realistic? By that, I mean do they conform to the real world which God presents to you today? Or have you fallen into the habit of asking for miracles that will relieve you of the necessity of struggle? So often, you and I are like the eighth-grader who chastised God for not granting her the miracle of a passing grade after she spent the semester watching television instead of studying. Like James and John, she wanted the glory while avoiding the pain.

"Can you drink of the cup I am to drink of?" Jesus asks each of us. The cup was the cup of suffering. Jesus detailed the ingredients of that chalice: the Son of Man will be handed over; the scribes and Pharisees will condemn him; the gentiles will mock him, flog him, and crucify him. Listen to Christ in the quiet moments of this Serious Season. He will lay out for you the full effects of your prayer. He will tell you that nothing worthwhile is ever won without a struggle. Though your cause be praiseworthy and your motives pure, the plan is God's. "Open your ears, O Christian people!" Hear not just the good news, but all the news.

> Thread of life unwinding,
>   swift the loom
>   tracing out
>   my desire.
> Simple is my figure:
>   peaceful heart,
>   loving home,
>   friendships true.
> Complex is God's weaving:
>   nub of doubt,
>   stitch of loss,
>   knot of pain.

> Colors in the shuttle:
>   green for hope,
>   white's new life,
>   golden age.
> Tapestry unfolding
>   God's design,
>   warp and woof,
>   day by day.
> Search the hidden pattern.
>   Take the time
>   to discern
>   His design.

Father, Guide and Goal, may we match our wants to your will. Transform the confusion of our lives into the pattern of your love. Help us to hear the whole of your Son's Good News. Amen.

THURSDAY OF THE SECOND WEEK

Abraham said to him, "If they do not listen to Moses and the prophets, they will not be convinced even if one should rise from the dead." (Lk 16:31)

The Bible is many things to many people. To those in mourning, words of consolation. To preachers, a book of insights. To church musicians, beautiful lyrics. To the scholar, a compendium of puzzles. To the Sunday School student, an assignment to be memorized. But for too many of us Christians, the Bible is a book of divine ideals impossible of accomplishment.

When Jesus tells the story of the rich man in the abode of the dead, he makes certain that his disciples understand his meaning. The Jewish scriptures, which embody the teachings of Moses and the prophets, are no more than a collection of dead letters if they are not put into practice. Without action, the word by itself has no power to save.

Lent is the season to get serious about the Bible. If you are not a daily Bible reader, now is the time to begin. A good start would be fifteen to twenty minutes a day, a minute or two to read a passage and the rest to listen to the Lord's commentary in silent meditation. But, beware! Bible reading can be dangerous to your present way of life. When Jesus told his disciples to listen to Moses and the prophets, he meant that they should heed the word of God. There is a great difference between hearing and heeding.

To "heed" the word means to "keep" the word, to let it take flesh in your life. If the thought of regular Bible reading frightens you, if you feel you lack the background to appreciate scriptural nuances, remember that Jesus put keeping the word above sophisticated understanding. The scribes and the Pharisees could recite the Bible backward and forward, but they were short on compassion, mercy, forgiveness, and tolerance.

Approach your Bible reading with the conviction that the Holy Spirit has something to say directly to you. Savor the words you have chosen for the day. Let them echo in your heart. They are God's message to you. Then, act on them. Put God's word into action in your world.

Daily Bible reading can be a source of immense joy and consolation. It can bring peace and hope to your heart. These ideals can be accomplished when you approach Holy Scripture expecting the words to come alive in your heart. After all, these words are the Word of God, the living Christ whose kingdom is alive and active. Alive in your heart. Active in your world.

> You have Moses and the prophets.
>
> They are dead, long gone, and useless,
> empty words on yellowed parchment,
> yearnings of another time.
>
> Listen to the age old wisdom.
>
> Myths and fables versus fact sheets?
> Shepherds, Temples, Ten Commandments,
> Tribes, and Pharaohs don't compute.
>
> Let My holy words instruct you.
>
> David's courage, Daniel's vision,
> Mary's "Yes," and Christ's compassion
> spring to life in each new day.
>
> Take My message to your people.
>
> In the silence of the hopeless
> sounds the step of Word-made-mercy,
> ancient Grace for hungry ears.

Father of Wisdom, open the treasure of your Holy Word to us. We long for your instruction and to hear your whispered Grace. Amen.

FRIDAY OF THE SECOND WEEK

When the chief priests and the Pharisees heard these parables, they realized he was speaking about them. Although they sought to arrest him they had reason to fear the crowds who regarded him as a prophet. (Mt 21:45-46)

If you have had the occasion to be a member of a crowd, you know that not only is there safety in numbers, there is power. Think of the noise at your last football game. In today's Gospel, Jesus finds safety from the chief priests and the Pharisees in the power of the crowds which approved him. Those who approve Jesus in the modern world often overlook the power at their disposal in mutual action. In fact, many Christians are loath to involve themselves in concerted efforts to right the wrongs of our society.

We live in a country which prizes the solitary hero or heroine. Much of the myth of America is built on the principle of rugged individualism and survival of the fittest. Our national anthem could be "I Did It My Way." As an idealistic young priest, I had the opportunity to see this self-protective ethic taken to its extreme. I was interviewing a young couple in preparation for the Baptism of their third child. They brought their four- and two-year old to the meeting. It was a perfect Norman Rockwell scene with each parent holding a child in place. For some reason the conversation turned to racial strife and open housing. The subject triggered a searing proclamation from the father to the effect that he would defend his home from declining property values with any means at his disposal. That's what his gun rack was for. My beautiful instruction on Baptism being a ceremony of welcome into the greater Christian family had apparently not registered.

Many people, including professing Christians, have no problem with letting the rest of the world go hang. Lent is the time to admit our failures to work with others for the greater good. Joint action by concerned Christians can free the power of the Holy Spirit that so many of us hold bound. Christians working together have closed down porn shops and abortion mills. Neighborhoods have been cleaned up and pagan public policies have been remedied. There is a danger, of course, when zealotry goes unchecked. Christians have abused the power of the crowd to the same degree that they have disregarded Christ's call for compassion and moderation. Only by recognizing the Beatitudes as everybody's Bill of Rights can we work together toward truly life-giving goals.

Take some time today to list the ongoing outrages against human dignity that you see in your community. Discuss them with like-minded women and men of various faiths. For every attack on decency and life, God has a plan for healing. In common prayer, ask him to show you and your friends his will in the matter. Then, slowly and deliberately work together to heal your neighborhood's wounds. The power to heal will be God's; the hands and hearts yours.

> The power of the Spirit flows
> in every yearning heart that knows
> how much it needs to hear the beat
> of other hearts to be complete.

It circulates, this power bound,
in timid whirlpools round and round
through turgid depth and rocky shoal
within my lonely landlocked soul.

The powerless beseech the Lord:
"Dear God, unsheathe your two-edged sword
to prick those hearts where Self has reigned
and free the rivers long constrained."

My heart so pierced by gentle grace
begins to bleed for this sad race.
Compassion is the stream that flows,
as every wounded healer knows.

The power of the Cross breaks free
when human solidarity
recalls the blood that makes us one
with God's Compassion, his own Son.

Father of the human family, let me not be an island in life's ocean. Make me, rather, a safe haven for the storm-tossed. With my brothers and sisters in Christian action, I will sweep the bright beam of your love across the dark seas.   Amen.

SATURDAY OF THE SECOND WEEK

Coming to his senses at last, he said: "How many hired hands at my father's place have more than enough to eat, while here I am starving! I will break away and return to my father."
(Lk 15:17-18)

During Lent, our loving Father gives us an opportunity to come to our senses in the same way the Prodigal Son did. The spark that turned this young man around occurred in his memory. It was a flicker of light that illumined a revealing scene long forgotten. He saw a picture in his mind of the hired hands' table groaning with food. "How many hired hands at my father's place have more than enough to eat." How generous was his father to give his employees more than they needed.

What brings you to ask God's forgiveness? Most would probably say that it is shame for their sins or confidence in the Father's forgiveness. But what must come before that? Why do your offenses against God make you ashamed in the first place? What is the basis of your confidence that you will be forgiven? It has to be your memory of God's goodness. If you weren't convinced of his past generosity, you would not dare to seek his pardon now. If you never saw God's love in your life, you could not be ashamed of betraying it. It is your memory of "more than enough" that brings you to your knees.

Today, meditate on all that God has given you and yours in the past. Think of yourself as the Prodigal Son. What is the spark of memory that would make you come to your senses? Dwell for a moment on when you were not, when you didn't exist. God's creative love gave you life. Without the generosity of God, you would not be. Think of those moments in your childhood when God's love became real for you in a parent's concern over your illness. How blessed you were to have someone to nurse you back to health. How about your adolescence — a time of storm and stress that tested to the limits the patience and spiritual stamina of your mother and father. Inspired by God's love, they did what they had to do and called you to maturity. Recall the blessings of your marriage. Who sent your husband or wife to you? God never wavered in his desire to send you "more than enough" love.

God loves you without let or hindrance. He has proved his love so often that it is hard to remember all the blessings. You know that he will prove it again with unconditional forgiveness. He has a track record of love that cannot fail to spark your memory of "more than enough."

> Why do we mark the tread of time
> with trauma, trial, and tears?
> > She died.
> > He broke.
> > War started.
>
> Is it because we will not bear
> the constant love of God
> > from which
> > we can't
> > be parted?
>
> His love illuminates our need,
> our thirst to be fulfilled.
> > We know
> > we are
> > half-hearted.
>
> By far, God's galaxy of grace
> outshines our dark recall,
> > the cold
> > bleak world
> > we've charted.
>
> So number not your blackest nights
> but count the mornings bright
> > with love
> > which God
> > imparted.

Good God, your blessings overwhelm me. Though I betray the gift, do not withdraw your grace from my life. Fill my need with your love and make me whole again. Amen.

THIRD SUNDAY OF LENT

> The hour was about noon. When a Samaritan woman came to draw water, Jesus said to her, "Give me a drink." (His disciples had gone off to the town to buy provisions.) The Samaritan woman said to him, "You are a Jew. How can you ask me, a Samaritan and a woman, for a drink?" (Recall that Jews have nothing to do with Samaritans.) (Jn 4:6-8)

Some years ago, the songwriter, Randy Newman, stirred up a great deal of controversy with his playful tune, "Short People." A surprising number of people who considered themselves below average height took exception to Newman's supposed slurs against their brothers and sisters of small stature. They demanded an apology. Instead, Newman explained that the lyrics weren't about them at all. He had written a tongue-in-cheek expose of prejudice in general. For that he would make no apology.

Had he lived two thousand years ago, Randy Newman could have as easily written songs called "Samaritan People," or "Female People," or "Gentile People" to chide upstanding Jews about their prejudices. To put it perhaps too bluntly, in order for Jews to consider themselves the Chosen, everybody else had to be the unchosen. A good Jew had to avoid even the slightest contact with non-Jews lest he be defiled. A respectable rabbi could not even converse familiarly with any woman outside his family be she Jew or Gentile.

Third Sunday of Lent

With the smugness that comes from two thousand years of supposed enlightenment, we bestow a sophisticated smirk upon our spiritual ancestors . . . until a contemporary critique such as "Short People" brings us up short. Lent is an appropriate time to count your prejudices. Whom do you look down upon: blacks, whites, reds, browns, yellows, men, women, children, elders, Southerners, Yankees, hillbillies, Canucks, high school dropouts, poor people, drunkards, junkies, liberals, conservatives, Holy Joes, atheists, Communists, Socialists, gays, straights, Protestants, Catholics, charismatics, Bible-thumpers, athletes, eggheads, the retarded, lepers, the Eastern establishment, wheeler-dealers, convicts, hippies, nuns, brothers, priests, immigrants, foreigners, white collars, blue collars, no-necks, rednecks? If this list doesn't include one of the groups you dislike, blame space limitations.

"Groups" is the key word in any definition of prejudice. We stereotype great gobs of humanity because of a flaw we perceive in a single representative. Quite often it isn't even our own experience that twists our attitudes, but a perception handed down to us by family or friends. Either way the result is the same: Short people or _____ people are no good because of the actions of one person or a small minority.

Did Jesus grow up with any prejudices? We do not know. It would be foolish to hazard a guess. But he was a child and a boy and a youth in a good Jewish home, a member of a family whose lifestyle was encompassed by the laws of the Old Testament, including, it must be supposed the oft-repeated strictures protecting the exclusivity of the Chosen People. What we do know is seen in today's Gospel: a rabbi from Nazareth speaks to a woman — not just any woman, but a despised Samaritan. To the horror of his disciples, Jesus demonstrates that she is not an ogre — a sinner, yes, but not an ogre.

This lesson is the same one that you and I learn when we deal with persons one-on-one. Under all the labels they are pretty much like us, burdened with their own set of prejudices. They also discover that we are not ogres. In basketball, one-on-one might be a good defense. In human relationships, one-on-one is the only way to break down defenses.

Absurd	You are
the word	the bar
of judgment	to concourse
that calls	for they
forth walls	obey
and latches	the jailer
the gate	and meet
with hate	to greet
for strangers.	each other.
To speak	Insane
with weak	this vain
suspicion	illusion
of those	for in
who pose	your thin
no danger	enclosure
to you	you'll find
is to	one mind
enchain them.	imprisoned.

Father of all mankind, you sent your Son to break down the barriers that keep us apart. May I have some part in freeing the stranger from the shackles of intolerance. Let me greet with a holy kiss those whom you have sent to be my brothers and sisters. Amen.

MONDAY OF THE THIRD WEEK

But Naaman went away angry, saying, "I thought that he would surely come out and stand there to invoke the Lord his God, and would move his hand over the spot, and thus cure the leprosy." (2 K 5:11)

    A young man studying for the priesthood was having a vocational crisis. Should he leave or stay in the seminary? He prayed long and hard for a sign. One night he gazed out the window lost in his continuing turmoil of choices. Suddenly a falling star blazed a bright trail to the earth. He took this to be a sign that he was to continue toward the priesthood. For the last fifteen years, I have never doubted my decision. But I learned long since that it had nothing to do with the falling star.

    I had been like Naaman in the Second Book of Kings, expecting God to intervene with the grand gesture I thought I deserved. Naaman was the commander of an army. His king esteemed him. If his leprosy was to be cured, it would be by the hands of God's mighty prophet. Instead, Elisha told him to go jump in the lake, seven times. Indignant at this common treatment, Naaman had to be argued into the cleansing by his servants. They pointed out that, since he was willing to do something extraordinary to effect a cure, he should be willing to do the simpler thing.

    That falling star was not the solution to my crisis. My questions were resolved over months and years of discerning God's gentle urgings. Prayer, Scripture reading, meditation, and the wise guidance of others were all part of the discernment process. God called me to the priesthood with whispers, not the trumpet blast my pride said I was owed.

    Lent is a time to listen for gentle whispers, to find God in everyday events. Perhaps because we let our egos run away with our common sense, we fail to recognize his daily revelations. Many of us make year-long preparations to visit a faraway shrine, yet overlook God's fingerprints on the mirror of life. The daily miracle of the Eucharist is a case in point. If Naaman were a modern Catholic, he might be told to go to daily Mass for seven days. Such a mundane solution to his problem would probably make him indignant, yet the Mass is the center of healing for our wounded world.

God wants to speak to you during these days. He wants you to know his will for you. You will hear him in the call of a robin come home. His breath moves the budding trees. His heart warms the burgeoning earth. His love beams in the smile of a friend. Falling stars are quite spectacular, but they don't happen every day. God happens every day.

> My soul is thirsting for the Lord.
> How long until I see his face?
> A week, a month
> without a sign.
> No prodigy, no oracle.
> I've searched the heavens, read the leaves,
> been faithful to my horoscope,
> done everything
> to make God speak
> in words that I
> can understand.
> But God speaks soft in shadowed tones:
> a purring cat, the snowflake's fall,
> a week, a month,
> a thousand signs
> to gently urge
> my heart aright.
> Take time, my friend, to hear the breeze.
> God calls each day in common tongues.

Speak, Lord, I wish to know your will. Save me from rushing round my world seeking a sign that fits my pride. Let me recognize your gentle call in everyday miracles. Amen.

TUESDAY OF THE THIRD WEEK

> Peter came up and asked Jesus, "Lord, when my brother wrongs me, how often must I forgive him? Seven times?" "No," Jesus replied, "not seven times; I say, seventy times seven times."
> (Mt 18:21-22)

Among the casualties of the renewal of the Church is the sacrament of Penance. There may be good reasons why people don't go to Confession with the same frequency and regularity as they did in the past, but sinning less is not one of them. The definition of sin may have been reworded in our day, but the offenses against God and neighbor are still the same. So is God's desire to forgive.

The life of Jesus was an expression of God's love for humankind. When he healed, consoled, sacrificed, and taught, he was perfectly reflecting his Father's concern for us. Jesus' answer to Peter in today's Gospel is no exception. Peter sought guidance concerning the requirements of forgiveness. Jesus' answer was not only a lesson for Peter, but a description of God's unlimited forgiveness.

The number seven was heavy with Jewish symbolism. It was a sign of perfection. Peter was asking if there were a point at which forgiveness becomes perfect, not necessarily seven times, but some specific point beyond which the duty to forgive comes to an end. In multiplying the seven by seventy, Jesus makes the number indefinite. No specific number of instances should bring forgiveness to an end.

Here, Jesus reflects his Father's desire to forgive us as well as giving us a standard of forgiveness.

When people stay away from the sacrament of Penance for a long time, they lose touch with God's limitless desire to forgive. If you go to Confession only twice a year, it would take you four years to find out that God's forgiveness is limitless (4 x 2 = 8 = 7 + 1). There is a dark side to this little joke. You are depriving yourself of many opportunities to meet God at his best. God yearns to forgive. He sent his Son to be Forgiveness-in-the-flesh. The inevitable death and taxes should be increased by one — sin. And "where sin increased, grace abounded all the more" (Rm 5:21 RSV). God wants to encounter us where we fail, and forgive us.

You are probably planning to go to Confession before Easter. Revise your plans and go twice during Lent. Go this week. Resume your habit of frequent Confession. Perhaps it was forced on you when you were young; now, you're the master. But your sins have also matured. And so has your need to know you have been forgiven, to hear a human voice speak precious words of absolution. That absolution comes from the limitless mercy of God. Tap that power more often.

> Contrite my heart before you, Lord.
> My sins make me ashamed.
> Disgusted by my senseless wrongs,
> myself I've humbly blamed.
>
> But dare I call them happy faults,
> these smudges on my soul?
> Your mercy welcomes not the sin
> but makes the sinner whole.

Unlimited Forgiveness seeks
to pour Himself upon
this heart of mine, this sullied gem,
to get thee, damned spot, gone.

Each time I fail, I come to You
to hear the words again,
those syllables of power and love
which cleanse me of the stain.

Father, pardon me, for I know well what I've done. May your infinite desire to forgive separate sin from sinner and make me whole again. Amen.

WEDNESDAY OF THE THIRD WEEK

Jesus said to his disciples: "Do not think that I have come to abolish the law and the prophets. I have come, not to abolish them, but to fulfill them." (Mt 5:17)

Can you imagine the reaction of Jesus' disciples to the above statement? They knew he was not talking about rigid adherence to every Jewish law and every prophetic teaching. They had already seen him break some religious laws for good reason. He healed on the Sabbath. He permitted his followers to pick grain for their daily sustenance on the Sabbath. They correctly understood Jesus to be saying that he was the fulfillment of the law and the prophets. All the prophets pointed to the coming of the Messiah. All the laws prepared for the Messiah. Jesus told his disciples that he was the One toward whom the prophets pointed and for whom the law prepared. That is why he later says that not the smallest letter of the law can be done away with until his Messiahship is recognized. The preparation and the pointing must continue until all men and women recognize him.

Now and then, you and I have trouble with one or another of the Church's laws. Perhaps we don't see the value in a fast day or a long marriage preparation process. Holy days of obligation sometimes can be very inconvenient. And why can't girls serve at the altar? Must we rigidly observe all these laws? After all, Christ has come. We don't need to cross every "t" and dot every "i" to prepare for him.

Yes, Christ has come. But not everyone recognizes him. Our example of obedience to the laws of the Church makes a powerful statement to those of our friends who will not accept Jesus Christ as their Savior. We all know people who would rather not see the open practice of religious obedience. It gets on their nerves, makes them question their lifestyles. It makes them think.

Jesus wanted his disciples to make people think about the fulfillment of their laws. In observing the laws of Judaism, his followers would be making a powerful statement of belief in the coming Messiah. Jesus wants us to make people think. By observing the laws of our Church, we are saying that Christ is among us and that he is here for all people.

How do you stand in relationship to the laws of the Church? Take some time today to examine your mission of obedience. Are you giving the powerful example that Jesus approves? Are you making people think?

>
> They watch you when you attend Church
> first
> out of wonder at your fervor
> then
> you begin to raise their hackles:

Why is she so strict about it?
First
she works hard at home and office
then
interrupts her rest to worship.

Is there something I am missing?
First
maybe I should meet my Pastor
then
after that I'll see what happens.

O Divine Lawgiver, make me more obedient to your law for my sake and the sake of my friends. Let them see in the practice of my faith that your Son truly lives among us. May his law of love become my law of life. Amen.

THURSDAY OF THE THIRD WEEK

Say to them: This is the nation which does not listen to the voice of the Lord, its God, or take correction. Faithfulness has disappeared; the word itself is banished from their speech. (Jr 7:28)

It seems that every day the news about the permanence of marriage is more disquieting. Last year, for every two marriages, there was one divorce. Religion is not immune to this loss of commitment. Although the rate has decreased, priests, sisters and brothers are still leaving their ministries. The rate of admissions to seminaries and religious houses declines steadily. Commitment seems to be passe.

The evidence in your life may not be so dramatic, yet

most of us have to admit an erosion in faithfulness. This is a season to get serious about a loss of religious resolve that has crept into our lives over the past year. Can you remember the resolutions you made last Lent? If you are like me, you promised God and yourself to pray more, to cultivate patience, to avoid overindulging, to be kinder to friends and more forgiving to foes. Whatever was on your list probably took a beating because at some point over the year you decided that it just wasn't worth it.

It didn't happen all at once, but your commitment began to waver when it became harder and harder to see any personal gain. The idea of personal gain is at the heart of most broken commitments: My prayers weren't answered. My patience was repaid with insult. My moderation made me nervous. My forgiveness made me look like a fool. In short, it began to seem that I wasn't getting anything out of it.

Commitment is not about personal gain. Commitment is for others. Your healthy prayer life makes you a better witness for Christ. Your patience brings peace to your friends. Your moderation helps others to see the right path. Your forgiveness is balm for another's wound. Healing a hurting marriage is the salvation of your spouse and children. The permanent sacrifice inherent in the priesthood and religious life is the salvation of the world.

Take a new look at the resolutions you've made for this Lent. See them as not so much for personal gain but as saving grace for those around you. Your commitment must be kept so that your relationships with others may become more fruitful, leading them to a new awareness of who they are and how much God loves them. This is the gain that your faithfulness brings to your world.

The promise kept
is God's own joy
if it is made for others.

To give your hope
for better days
to those whose roads are rutted

makes them aware
that they can strive
to walk upon the uplands.

So promise hope
to all who fail
to see God's light in darkness

by holding true
to what you've pledged.
Your gain is their salvation.

Faithful Father, I know you believe in me and are committed to my happiness. Help me to keep my promises to you and to your children. Let my fidelity to your way be a beacon in their darkness. Amen.

FRIDAY OF THE THIRD WEEK

One of the scribes came up to Jesus and asked him,
"Which is the first of all the commandments?" Jesus replied:
"This is the first:
    'Hear, O Israel! The Lord our God is Lord alone!
    Therefore, you shall love the Lord your God
        with all your heart,
        with all your soul,
        with all your mind,
        and with all your strength.'
    This is the second,
        'You shall love your neighbor as yourself.' " (Mk 12:28-31)

Do you love yourself? Oh, I know you are good to yourself. You pamper yourself, make yourself comfortable, and try to structure your life so you won't be inconvenienced. But do you love yourself?

The answer to this question is of more than passing interest when it comes to living out Jesus' command to love our neighbor. He makes love of self the standard of our love for others. Too many of us don't really love ourselves. We are dissatisfied with the way we look or with our level of intelligence. We carry within us deep scars from past failures. We blame ourselves, and rightly so, for the evil that we do; but even though God had forgiven us, we can't forgive ourselves.

Much of this self-hate is unconscious, but it can be seen by others in our relationships. The psychological phenomenon of projection gives us away. The things we dislike in ourselves, even unconsciously, are projected to others. We think we see in them the traits that disgust us in ourselves. Because we distrust our deepest emotions, we may avoid people who become emotional easily. Because we are avaricious, we think everyone is out to get the better part of our pocketbooks. Because we have a tendency to distort the truth, we believe very little of what others say.

Now, Jesus tells us that we must love others as we love ourselves. Logic demands a change in our own self-appraisal because Jesus wants us to love others as much as we love God — with all our heart, soul, mind and strength. That's how much Jesus loved his sisters and brothers, and we are to be like him. Therefore, we must increase our love for ourselves to match his love for others.

During Lent, when we have resolved to be better persons, we should concentrate on our virtues as well as on our faults. Chances are good that we will find more to rejoice over than weep about. Take some time to note and give thanks for the goodness God has placed in you. Remember, God doesn't make junk.

the shadows in me cloud my vision make me see the dark side	the Son shines in me cleansing my sight brightening my good side
of every brother all my sisters suffering from my sins	washing my brothers and each sister clean of all my own sins
they are as bad as I think I am hiding base and vile thought	they are as good as God has made me enfleshment of His thought

Creator of all good, my soul is your divine spark of life. Fan it to a flame which will consume all dark thoughts of self so that I may see reflected in my own brightness the goodness of your sons and daughters. Amen.

SATURDAY OF THE THIRD WEEK

He will revive us after two days:
   on the third day he will raise us up,
      to live in his presence.

> Let us know, let us strive to know the Lord;
>   as certain as the dawn is his coming,
>   and his judgment shines forth like
>   the light of day!
> He will come to us like the rain,
>   like spring rain that waters the earth. (Hos 6:2-3)

Lent has two themes. It is a season of penance and a season of preparation. The prophet Hosea reminds us of what we are preparing for. Although the Old Testament references to "two days" and "the third day" have the meaning of "a little while," we Christians see in these terms a definite foreshadowing of the death and resurrection of Jesus. While the purification of penance is one way of making ready for the Easter celebration, to be complete it must be complemented by hopeful anticipation.

Hopeful anticipation is embodied in a firm belief that Christ will come again in glory and that the beginning of that glory is the Resurrection. "As certain as the dawn is his coming." How many days in your life have been without the dawn? Those are the odds against Christ's glory.

How does this firm belief show forth in your life? "Let us strive to know the Lord." The purification of penance is the prelude to your invitation to Jesus to come and dwell with you. You clean the house before you ask the guest to enter. Your purpose is to know Jesus better by living in his presence.

It is true that we are always in the presence of the risen Christ. But we must strive to recognize him in our lives. His presence is not that of spectacle or prodigy; rather, he comes to us "like spring rain that waters the earth." Just as the farmer anticipates the spring rain which brings new life to the frozen earth, so we cultivate hopeful anticipation of Christ's Easter triumph.

Saturday of the Third Week

Today, meditate on the future. Think seriously about Lent as a prologue to a wonderful story, a story of new life, of the Firstborn from the dead who shares his new life with all who desire his presence. Lent does not stand alone. It is *for* something. Think about what that something is for you. Let your hopeful anticipation be seen in cheerful words and deeds. Share your future.

> The promise of springtime
> disturbs the sleeping seed.
> A new life is stirring
> awake the frozen reed.
>
> A season of shadows
> gives way to crescent sun.
> The earth's resurrection
> at long last has begun.
>
> Man's hope for the future
> bound tightly in the cave
> is sighing and stretching
> against the icy grave.
>
> A crack in the great stone
> emits a shaft of light
> which touching the dark world
> begins the end of night.

Father of all our hopes, you have planted the seed of anticipation in our hearts. Teach us how to nurture this holy longing so that we may welcome the fruit of your mercy and love. At the end of this sacred season, may our harvest be new life for the world. Amen.

FOURTH SUNDAY OF LENT

When Jesus heard of his expulsion, he sought him out and asked him, "Do you believe in the Son of Man?" He answered, "Who is he, sir, that I may believe in him?" "You have seen him," Jesus replied. "He is speaking to you now." "I do believe, Lord," he said, and bowed down to worship him. Then Jesus said:
"I came into this world to divide it,
to make the sightless see
and the seeing blind." (Jn 9:35-39)

Many of us are troubled by Biblical passages about Jesus which do not fit into our assessment of his personality and mission. When he says that he will bring not peace, but a sword or when he predicts that his teaching will divide mother and daughter, son and father, we feel uneasy. Such statements should not fall from the gentle lips of the Good Shepherd, the Suffering Servant, the Lamb of God. In today's Gospel, Jesus said, "I came into this world to divide it," and we experience that familiar sinking feeling.

Our reluctance to accept the complete message of Jesus is evidence of our inability to believe that anything good can come from adversity. A glance at television commercials will illustrate our impatience with even the slightest discomfort. Whether it be a headache or underarm odor, we need not endure it for another second. To continue to live with unease, to believe in the fruits of adversity seems almost un-American.

When Jesus says he will divide families and nations, he is stating the obvious. Not everyone will agree with his teaching; suspicion, opposition, and adversity will result. Not that he wills division; rather, as a wise observer of human nature he knows what will happen. His encouragement of prayer,

Fourth Sunday of Lent

fortitude, and faith are meant to strengthen his followers so that they may endure the inevitable trial and harvest the fruits of adversity.

This harvest is seen clearly in today's Gospel. Consider the evolution of the newly-sighted man's faith as he is confronted with the kind of attack most dreaded by a good Jew: a cross-examination by the Pharisees.

The first to question him were plain people like himself. Compared to the Pharisees, they threw him creampuffs. Who opened his eyes? "That man they call Jesus. . . ." His faith was still latent. It was just a man. Then they took him to the Pharisees who pointed out that this man called Jesus must be a sinner because he healed on a Sabbath. The newly-sighted man now experienced an increase of faith. "He is a prophet," he said of the One who healed him. After questioning his parents, the Pharisees came back to the man and resumed the cross-examination. They made the matter a test of the man's faith in God Almighty. "Give glory to God." Tell the truth and honor God! They made him repeat the story, but each time he refused to label Jesus as a sinner. "If this man were not from God, he could never have done such a thing." At this, they expelled him from their midst, and, presumably, from the synagogue. No worse adversity could befall the faithful Jew.

Yet, after all this, when Jesus told him that he was the Son of Man, the man said, "I do believe, Lord," and worshipped him as the Messiah. Adversity had borne fruit. Every test had brought with it a greater capacity for belief, from Jesus as "that man" to "prophet" to "Lord." Adversity had called forth not merely endurance, but growth in faith.

Think of this progression as you struggle with your daily crosses and question the worth of the added Lenten penances you have taken on. This Serious Season, like your life, is not something merely to be endured. There is a triumph waiting for you at the end of Lent, a triumph foreshadowing what will be yours at the end of your life, if you take advantage of the opportunities for growth which always accompany adversity.

>Faith on satin pillows.
>Hope in God's blind rescue.
>Charity at arm's length.
>Hail to easy virtue!

>Where is the refiner's purifying fire?
>Where is the investment growth and grit require?

>Faith demands commitment.
>Hope endures the set-to.
>Love is proved in absence.
>Blest the tested virtue!

>Here the saints and martyrs suffered on the way.
>Here the Savior's Passion calls to Easter Day.

Father of mercy, I have not the courage to seek adversity, but I know it will come riding on life's shoulders. Help me to endure my trials and walk more surely in the footsteps of him who was mankind's Wounded Healer. As he was perfected through suffering, let me grow from strength to strength, from virtue to virtue, from glory to glory. Amen.

MONDAY OF THE FOURTH WEEK

"Sir," the royal official pleaded with him, "come down before my child dies." Jesus told him, "Return home. Your son will live." The man put his trust in the word Jesus spoke to him, and started for home. (Jn 4:49-50)

Monday of the Fourth Week

Trust in the Lord is the keystone of Lenten purification. The first step in purification is examination. We must make an inventory of our lives to determine what belongs and what does not. As we proceed through this sometimes painful process, we will turn over some rocks that have not been disturbed for many months. When the sin hiding beneath the rock is revealed, we are justly ashamed. But what of the Lord? What is his reaction? Will he share our disgust? We must trust that he will not. Jesus' love for us is not diminished by our sins. Without condoning the evil we have done, Jesus understands better than we what led up to our foolish act. We trust Jesus to be Jesus, the Lord whose mission was precisely to make us whole again, to assist us in reintegrating those parts of us which have regressed to a childish state. God's Love Incarnate cannot help loving us. His love makes us whole. We trust that love.

The next step in our purification is confession. We must trust Jesus to forgive us. How many are the lonely souls who confess again and again one single incident of sin long past because they have recurring doubts about the Lord's willingness to forgive? Tortured by lack of trust, they imagine themselves to be more powerful in their sinfulness than Jesus is in his forgiveness. We must trust that there is nothing we could possibly do that Christ is not willing to forgive. The only "unforgivable sin" is our doubt that Jesus wants to forgive. If we don't believe in his desire to welcome us back, we won't take the first step to return to him. Trust that Jesus is waiting, like the Prodigal Son's father, for you to return.

Finally, convinced that Jesus loves us even though we are sinners, and trusting in his willingness to forgive, we believe that his capacity to pardon is inexhaustible. With the fickleness of children, we may commit the same sin tomorrow that was forgiven today. After days or weeks of painful self-examination, after the shame of admitting our sin to ourselves and to the Lord, after the exhiliration of being forgiven, we do it again. We must trust that we will again be forgiven. Purification is a process, a journey to wholeness. There are times in our lives when the backward steps outnumber the forward. Jesus walks beside us even when we march full speed to the rear. He wants to keep very close to us so that we won't have to wait for his forgiveness. Today, do no less than the royal official. Put your trust in the healing word Jesus speaks to you.

> Of course the Lord is powerful.
> Observe his grand design,
> the sky above, the earth below,
> and all things yours and mine.
> He fashioned each of us from dust,
> sustains us every day.
> To what can I compare his might?
> No force stands in his way
> except the evil that I do,
> for I am god of sin.
> He cannot conquer my mistrust
> of his desire that in
> my soul his all-forgiving touch
> might bring the balm of peace.
> O foolish one, he gently chides,
> I've come with sweet release.
> Your deeds may be as black as night,
> your conscience raw and sore,
> but trust me now to pardon you,
> to make you whole once more.

Monday of the Fourth Week

Trust in the Lord is the keystone of Lenten purification. The first step in purification is examination. We must make an inventory of our lives to determine what belongs and what does not. As we proceed through this sometimes painful process, we will turn over some rocks that have not been disturbed for many months. When the sin hiding beneath the rock is revealed, we are justly ashamed. But what of the Lord? What is his reaction? Will he share our disgust? We must trust that he will not. Jesus' love for us is not diminished by our sins. Without condoning the evil we have done, Jesus understands better than we what led up to our foolish act. We trust Jesus to be Jesus, the Lord whose mission was precisely to make us whole again, to assist us in reintegrating those parts of us which have regressed to a childish state. God's Love Incarnate cannot help loving us. His love makes us whole. We trust that love.

The next step in our purification is confession. We must trust Jesus to forgive us. How many are the lonely souls who confess again and again one single incident of sin long past because they have recurring doubts about the Lord's willingness to forgive? Tortured by lack of trust, they imagine themselves to be more powerful in their sinfulness than Jesus is in his forgiveness. We must trust that there is nothing we could possibly do that Christ is not willing to forgive. The only "unforgivable sin" is our doubt that Jesus wants to forgive. If we don't believe in his desire to welcome us back, we won't take the first step to return to him. Trust that Jesus is waiting, like the Prodigal Son's father, for you to return.

Finally, convinced that Jesus loves us even though we are sinners, and trusting in his willingness to forgive, we believe that his capacity to pardon is inexhaustible. With the fickleness of children, we may commit the same sin tomorrow that was forgiven today. After days or weeks of painful self-examination, after the shame of admitting our sin to ourselves and to the Lord, after the exhiliration of being forgiven, we do it again. We must trust that we will again be forgiven. Purification is a process, a journey to wholeness. There are times in our lives when the backward steps outnumber the forward. Jesus walks beside us even when we march full speed to the rear. He wants to keep very close to us so that we won't have to wait for his forgiveness. Today, do no less than the royal official. Put your trust in the healing word Jesus speaks to you.

> Of course the Lord is powerful.
> Observe his grand design,
> the sky above, the earth below,
> and all things yours and mine.
> He fashioned each of us from dust,
> sustains us every day.
> To what can I compare his might?
> No force stands in his way
> except the evil that I do,
> for I am god of sin.
> He cannot conquer my mistrust
> of his desire that in
> my soul his all-forgiving touch
> might bring the balm of peace.
> O foolish one, he gently chides,
> I've come with sweet release.
> Your deeds may be as black as night,
> your conscience raw and sore,
> but trust me now to pardon you,
> to make you whole once more.

Almighty God, increase my trust in your desire and power to forgive. You gave your message of mercy to our world in the Person of your beloved Son. Say but the word and we shall be healed. Amen.

TUESDAY OF THE FOURTH WEEK

There was a man who had been sick for thirty-eight years. Jesus, who knew he had been sick a long time, said when he saw him lying there, "Do you want to be healed?" "Sir," the sick man answered, "I don't have anyone to plunge me into the pool once the water has been stirred up. By the time I get there, someone else has gone in ahead of me." Jesus said to him, "Stand up! Pick up your mat and walk!" The man was immediately cured; he picked up his mat and began to walk. (Jn 5:5-9)

In Jerusalem there was a pool near the Sheep Gate whose waters were thought to have curative powers. This healing power was especially effective when new water entered the pool from its underground spring. The spring made the water bubble up, and the first person able to get into the pool during the movement of the water supposedly had the best chance for a cure.

All around the pool sat the infirm, including the man in the Gospel who was so ill that he never got to the pool before the movement stopped. Jesus saw his plight and cured him on the spot.

There is a nursing home in our community that reminds me of this story. Many of its residents are bedridden; others are confined to wheelchairs. All suffer in one degree or another the rigors of age. Since age is the one disease that cannot be healed, no one is able to take these seniors to any kind of healing pool. All are in the same fix as the man in the

Gospel. There is nothing that can reverse or even halt the ravages of time.

There are several churches and service groups that send members to visit this home. There, they do the work of Jesus. Since there is no place of healing to which the old can be taken, these generous visitors bring Christ's healing love to them. Even though the body wears out, the soul can retain its youth when the therapy of sharing is prescribed.

There is probably a home like this in your community. Some of the residents receive regular visits from family members, but others have no families. Make some inquiries about the latter. Find out if there is a way to adopt a grandparent. Make it your mission to bring the water of life, Christ's healing touch, to a lonely soul.

> Above his head a calendar hung:
> two kids playing with a puppy,
> the seal of a full-service bank,
> and thirty-one January dates.
>
> Nothing else hung on the walls
> but kids, puppy, bank,
> and dates, small in large squares,
> to permit the writing of a note.
>
> The gnarled hand bade me come closer,
> then pointed painfully up,
> not to kids, puppy, or bank,
> but to the spidery words.
>
> By what effort could he have reached
> high enough to scrawl in crayon
> on Sunday, the seventh:
> Last visit from son.
>
> My tears made me turn away
> and move for a moment
> to the wide-open window.
> I drank in the fresh April air.

Father of life, you sent your Son to heal the sick and comfort the broken-hearted. Show me where the hurt is deepest, and there, with him, I shall go. Amen.

WEDNESDAY OF THE FOURTH WEEK

> The Father himself judges no one but has assigned all judgment to the Son, so that all men may honor the Son just as they honor the Father. (Jn 5:22-23)

This is a season to think seriously about judgment. Because they fear the wrath of God, many would rather think of anything but God's estimation of them. Jesus' statement about judgment in today's Gospel seems, at first glance, to confuse the issue. If I am to go to all the trouble and endure all the trepidation involved in meditating on how I stand with God, don't mix me up by telling me that God has assigned judgment to Jesus.

However, if you make a slight adjustment in your reasoning, this can be a very reassuring meditation. Think of God not as assigning judgment to Jesus but as making Jesus his judgment upon humankind. See Jesus as God's judgment-made-flesh. Jesus is the incarnation of what God thinks of you and me.

Jesus is God's love for all men and women. He sent his Son to show us how much he loved us. What does God think of you? He considers you infinitely valuable. Only a Divine Person could assure you of this loving judgment. He considers you reasonable, able to tell truth from falsehood. Only One of limitless knowledge could convince you of his Way. He considers you capable of answering "Yes" to his call. Only One with sublime attractiveness would be good enough to offer the invitation. He considers you striving to turn away from sin. Only One bearing absolute forgiveness could pardon you. He considers you an eminently fit companion for him in heaven. Only One who shares his Godhead could make you aware of his friendship. And finally, he considers you worth dying for. Only the ultimate sacrifice of his beloved Son would suffice to reveal your true value.

Yes, God has made his judgment upon you in Jesus Christ. You have nothing to fear when Jesus is judgment. From all eternity God has esteemed you worthy, valuable, lovable, a friend. This day, give thanks to him for not leaving you in the dark about yourself. You are the apple of his eye. He would do anything for you. He has done everything for you.

Which one of us
would ever dream
that we are held
in such esteem?

Instead, he sends
his judgment, love
made flesh and blood,
and smiles above.

We know our faults;
we know them well.
There seems no room
for pride to swell.

He values us
much more than we
conceive our own
true worth to be.

Almighty God,
in justice true,
could sentence us
to endless rue.

If this great God
can love us so,
are not we worth
more than we know?

Just Judge, we praise you for your goodness. In your Son, Jesus Christ, we see our noble lineage. He is your judgment of love upon us. Thank you for showing us how valuable we are to you. May we follow in his footsteps and fulfill your hope in us.   Amen.

THURSDAY OF THE FOURTH WEEK

But Moses implored the Lord, his God, saying, "Why, O Lord, should your wrath blaze up against your own people, whom you brought out of the land of Egypt with such great power and with so strong a hand?" (Ex 32:11)

When the priest went into his church one evening to lock the doors, he heard a strange sound. He walked toward the altar, and there in the dim light he saw an old lady, a stranger to him, kneeling in front of the statue of the Sacred Heart. Her voice rose and fell, sometimes a mutter, then quite distinct. Since she gave no sign of noticing him, he stopped and listened. He heard snatches of sentences: "Why didn't you . . . don't you remember that I told you . . . sick and tired of being. . . ." Feeling like an eavesdropper, he cleared his throat and approached the woman. Startled, she turned to him and saw the keys in his hand. "Father," she said, "can you give me a few more minutes? I'm not finished arguing with him yet."

Arguing with the Lord is an ancient tradition most of us have lost track of. The first reading from the Book of Exodus is just one example of many in the Old Testament where Moses and other holy men and women implore, cajole, debate, and, yes, argue with God. In the New Testament, we can see Mary's demurrer, "How can this be? I know not man," as a statement, albeit momentary, of her desire to draw God's attention to the unreasonableness of his messenger's announcement. And again, we see an equally brief statement of opposition to God's plan when Jesus, in the Garden of Gethsemane, asks that the cup of suffering might pass from him.

Perhaps arguing with God is a lost art today because of an overemphasis on spiritual docility. Spiritual writers tell us to wait, to discern, to let God speak to us. These attitudes are commendable if evoked in moderation. There are times when it is quite healthy to plead our cause before the Divine Planner, not that we tell God something he doesn't already know, but for the sake of our own spiritual dignity. We were created to think, speak and act. If *every* time we come before our Maker in prayer, we repress these faculties which he gave us, we fail to exercise our rights as beings of reason and ardor. God gave us emotions so we could be passionate, passionate about decisions and events that are of vital importance to us. He wants us to know what we want. Take some time today to tell yourself exactly what you want. Then tell God.

> When I pray I say:
> Let it be this way.
> God knows best for me
> but it's hard to see
> when he's turned his back
> how he can keep track
> of my every need
> in the life I lead.
>
> Listen, Lord, I cry,
> don't forget that my
> very life's at stake
> in the plans you make.
> Come around, please do.
> See my point of view.
> Your plan may be best.
> Let's give mine a test.

Guide and Goal of my life, hear my plea. Pour out your blessings upon me in ways I understand. Fill my cup with joy, not sorrow. Let me feel the force of your love in the things of your creation. Amen.

FRIDAY OF THE FOURTH WEEK

The Jewish feast of Booths drew near. Once his brothers had gone up to the festival he too went up, but as if in secret and not for all to see. (Jn 7:2, 10)

Jesus came in secret to Jerusalem. It was the feast of Booths, the autumn harvest festival, a time when great crowds from the hinterland would converge on the City of Peace. The crowds were not always so peaceful. This greatest of Jewish feasts had been in the past the occasion for nationalistic uprisings. With so many people jamming the city, a tiny spark could set off a revolt. Jesus didn't want to be that spark. He stayed behind until his "brothers" left for the feast. These brothers were not his disciples but members of his extended family who thought they saw in him a leader of revolt. Jesus purposely let them go ahead of him so as not to encourage their rebellious plans.

You and I are often led into spiritually dangerous situations by those we consider our friends. We know they gossip, but we fall in with their critical conversations. We know they drink too much, and still we try to match them glass for glass. We know they swear and curse, so we delete not one expletive. We know they are attracted to immoral entertainments, so we buy a ticket and take a seat. We know they break their marriage vows, so we bend ours a bit.

It takes courage to let our brothers and sisters go on without us. It takes courage to be left alone. It takes the courage of Christ. Today, we ask God to give us that courage, not only for our own sake but for the salvation of our friends.

When we are absent from these dangerous situations, there is one less person to stir the pot. Our absence is noticed and remarked. Party-pooper or Holy Joe or Jane isn't there.

Deep down, somebody will ask herself or himself, why? That may well be the first of a series of questions which lead to another person dropping out of the club. God even works through your absence.

There is no Biblical evidence that any of the brothers who went to Jerusalem without Jesus asked himself why the Master was absent. But it is certainly reasonable to believe that some of them eventually became his true disciples because he would not permit them to make him a rebel chieftain. Instead of Jesus in their midst at the festival, they were faced with a question mark that demanded an answer. Take a serious look at your friends this season. Would some of them be better off at a gathering that included not you but a question mark?

> We noticed you weren't there last night.
> We had a lot of fun.
> The midnight hour had come and gone.
> We still were on the run.
>
> What prompted you to chicken out?
> The party was the best,
> except, of course, that you weren't there.
> I guess you need your rest.
>
> If I told you why I stayed home,
> you'd laugh at what I said.
> Suffice to say, my friend, I sent
> a question mark instead.

Heavenly Father, be my companion on the lonely road of righteousness. Give me the courage to be your Son's true disciple by turning the thoughts of others to him. Show me where my absence will reveal his presence. Amen.

SATURDAY OF THE FOURTH WEEK

I knew their plot because the Lord informed me; at that time you, O Lord, showed me their doings. Yet I, like a trusting lamb led to slaughter, had not realized that they were hatching plots against me: "Let us destroy the tree in its vigor; let us cut him off from the land of the living, so that his name will be spoken no more."
But, you, O Lord of hosts, O just Judge,
   searcher of mind and heart,
Let me witness the vengeance you take on them,
   for to you I have entrusted my cause! (Jr 11:18-20)

"Don't get mad, get even," says the smart operator. It seems that Jeremiah wanted it both ways. He certainly got angry, and who wouldn't? He was using his prophetic charism to lambaste those Jews who were worshipping at pagan shrines in the area. He even had a plan to tear the shrines down. The plot that so incensed him was concocted by townspeople who may have included members of his immediate family. They wanted to do away with him so the shrine wouldn't be disturbed. He got mad and asked God to get even.

Jeremiah lived long before Jesus told his followers to turn the other cheek. Perfect charity was not a part of Jeremiah's religion. Various Old Testament stories include scenes of bloody vengeance. An eye for an eye and a tooth for a tooth was a natural attitude for a people who had, at best, only a hazy idea of an afterlife. Things had to be balanced in this world, and Yahweh, the just Judge, was just the God to do it.

We suppose ourselves to be more enlightened in our day. We would never think of demanding that God punish someone who hurt us. Instead, we do it ourselves. Children are quite open about it: "She hit me first." "He took my pen." We adults are more circumspect. The cold shoulder, the cutting remark, the spiteful gossip are our weapons, and we wield them with the skill of a surgeon. "Justice demands an answer to insult," we say. But is it God's justice or ours?

Jesus is the personification of God's justice. He taught us to overcome enmity with love, to startle our foes by returning a blessing instead of a curse, to win by appearing to lose. Today, look to those in your life from whom you are separated by the barrier of your home-grown justice. Then don't get mad and don't get even. Get together.

> The trouble with getting
> even
> is that it means getting
> above
> by trying to put one
> over
> on someone who put you
> down.
>
> If we weren't so unsure
> inside
> and so righteous on the
> outside
> we could forget what comes
> between
> ourselves and those we live
> among.

God of justice, deal with me not as I deserve but as your Son dealt with his tormentors. His justice was to bless. Help me to pour the same justice of Jesus upon the heads of those who injure me. Amen.

FIFTH SUNDAY OF LENT

Martha said to Jesus, "Lord, if you had been here, my brother would never have died. Even now, I am sure that God will give you whatever you ask of him." "Your brother will rise again," Jesus assured her. "I know he will rise again," Martha replied, "in the resurrection on the last day." Jesus told her:
> "I am the resurrection and the life:
> whoever believes in me,
> though he should die, will come to life;
> and whoever is alive and believes in me
> will never die.
> Do you believe this?"

"Yes, Lord," she replied. "I have come to believe that you are the Messiah, the Son of God: he who is to come into the world."
(Jn 11:21-27)

I was brought up on the Baltimore Catechism — Blue, Green, and Red — the whole rainbow of rote memorization. In religion class, I shined brighter than the North Star; memorization was my forte. So, if Jesus had attempted to comfort me with the same words he addressed to Martha in today's Gospel, I am afraid my reply would have been as inappropriate as hers.

Just as I repeated words in religion class without grasping their real meaning, so Martha's words betray her inability to fathom the mystery that is Jesus. When he tells her that her brother will rise again, she repeats the standard formula taught by those Jews who believed in a final resurrection, principally the Pharisees: "I know he will rise again in the resurrection on the last day."

In answer, Jesus says, "I am the resurrection and the life." He does not promise resurrection. He does not say resurrection will come through him. He does not point to the last day. He says he *is* the resurrection. He *is* that mystery which conquers death. Martha is in the presence of the Resurrection and all the lessons she has ever learned, all the Scripture passages she knows by heart, all the praying she has ever done fall woefully short of encompassing the mystery that is Jesus.

Whoever dies believing in the mystery that is Jesus will come to life. Whoever is alive and believes shall never die. Martha's schoolbook faith must be expanded a hundredfold to receive the essence of the Good News: this Jesus who stands before her is the completion of the Law and the prophets. He raises all belief to the level of personal experience. And he transforms the hope for a final resurrection, which was so tentative in Martha's day, into a present reality. Resurrection begins in the presence of Jesus. It can be experienced by the living who come close to him. It is this promise fulfilled that Jesus speaks of when he asks Martha, and you and me, "Do you believe this?"

When Martha says, "Yes, Lord, I have come to believe that you are the Messiah, the Son of God: he who is to come into the world," she responds to the power of Jesus drawing her upward into the mystery of his person. The Pharisees' teachings about a final resurrection now fade into the background. They have become rudimentary stepping stones which were useful in bridging the gap between hope and realization. At this moment, Martha has crossed over to the uplands where she will see her brother, Lazarus, alive again. The presence of Jesus, the mystery of Jesus, the power of Jesus will make it so.

Each of us can look back on portions of our religious education with some amusement. Some of the teachings sound quite naive in the context of today's complex society. But no matter of what era, this training provided the stepping stones necessary to progress to a more mature faith. If

Fifth Sunday of Lent

you value your traditions and your teachers, as I do mine, then, today, honor both by examining your progress. Are you still plodding along the path of rote answers and simple solutions? To appreciate the real meaning of Lent and Easter, you must move to the uplands. Christ calls you into his presence, into his now. "I am the resurrection and the life." You cannot know the resurrection, you cannot know the life, until you know him.

> The answers that
> I love to hear
> are black and white
> and crystal clear.
>
> They don't slip through
> my porous mind
> but grab and hold
> as God designed.

So then I take my mind with me and plunge into humanity.
There in the moil of right and wrong my dogma seems not to belong.
Simplicity and chaos meet. My answers pat sound sad retreat.
Not black or white, but misty gray, this fog of choice obscures my way.

> O, for a voice
> of wisdom true
> that tells not what
> but whispers Who.
>
> This Answer walks
> beside me now,
> the Word made flesh,
> just I and Thou.

Holy Spirit of Wisdom, quiet my soul in the daily babble of contending voices. Guide me to that place of holy silence which signals the presence of Christ. Let me hear him and his message of continual resurrection. Amen.

MONDAY OF THE FIFTH WEEK

> But Susanna cried aloud: "O eternal God, you know what is hidden and are aware of all things before they come to be: you know that they have testified falsely against me. Here I am about to die, though I have done none of the things with which these wicked men have charged me." (Dn 13:42-44)

If there are black lies and white lies, Susanna, the heroine of today's passage from the Book of Daniel, was to be the victim of a black lie, a perversion of truth so grievous that it could result in her death. But like the U.S. Cavalry, Daniel comes to her rescue and proves the testimony of her accusers false. As it turns out, the two old men, who accused her of adultery as their revenge for her refusal to give in to their own lust, are themselves the victims of the fate they chose for her.

When we speak falsely, the chances are that we ourselves will reap the whirlwind. Our fate will not be as dramatic as that of Susanna's accusers for our lies are not as black. We specialize in white lies; we bend the truth or keep something back in order to give a false impression. For this we are not hauled before a court of justice or cross-examined by a prophetic district attorney. Our punishment is more subtle; sometimes we don't even notice it. It is called a lack of credibility.

After enough people have noticed that we play fast and

loose with the truth, we begin to suffer from a credibility gap. People become accustomed to taking our utterances with a grain of salt. They fall into the habit of double-checking everything we say. There was a little girl who delighted in her first watch. She longed for adults to ask her the time. But she was mischievous and began to answer that it was ten minutes later than it really was. She liked to see them jump and run to catch the bus or begin Mass. Quite soon no one asked her the hour anymore, even when she stooped to asking them if they wanted to know what time it was.

Check yourself today to see if you have a credibility gap. Do you invent excuses for your failings? Perhaps you distort the truth about a friend to add spice to a story. Did you really earn all those degrees? Did you come home late last night? How many times did you try to call me? All white lies. Nothing serious. Nobody got hurt. Except you.

> The structure of trust
> is fragile at best;
> thin lines
> of truth
> hold it
> steady.
>
> It doesn't take much
> to cause it to crack;
> one lie
> or two
> start it
> shaking.
>
> Now multiply that
> by falsehoods each day;
> white, black,
> and gray
> make it
> weaker.
>
> Before long the shock
> of total collapse
> surely
> will send
> your friends
> fleeing.

Father of all truth, cleanse my lips of falsehood so that I may be believed. Let my honest discourse be a fitting thanksgiving for the gift of speech. May I bring to life in my world your Word-made-flesh, Jesus Christ, our Lord.   Amen.

TUESDAY OF THE FIFTH WEEK

> You belong to what is below;
> I belong to what is above.
> You belong to this world —
> a world which cannot hold me.
> That is why I said you would die in your sins.
> You will surely die in your sins
> unless you come to believe that I AM.   (Jn 8:23-24)

What would you do if you walked into a church during a revival or a mission and the guest preacher began by saying that he was the embodiment of all your hopes, the one who had been promised for as long as your nation existed, and ended his sermon by saying that he was divine? You would either depart quickly or call the mental health clinic or both.

When Jesus used the term "I AM" about himself, he knew the Pharisees would recall Exodus 3:14. That is the same term that God used to identify himself to Moses at the burning bush. Moses wanted to be able to tell his people the name of the One he was speaking to. God said, "Tell them I AM sent you." This became the name of God for the Chosen People, a name so sacred that they were forbidden to pronounce it. We know it in Hebrew as "Yahweh." Now this carpenter's son, this itinerant preacher was calling himself by the same name God gave to himself. Would you be surprised if the Pharisees' reaction was the same as yours in that church?

We are precisely ten days away from that dark Friday afternoon when the One who called himself "I AM" will die on a cross. He won't look much like the embodiment of our hopes then. He will look like a man exhausted by torture and disappointment, a man without friends, seemingly bereft of hope. But above all, he will look like a man.

It would be fitting to meditate today on the divinity of Jesus. Upon the cross will hang the Second Person of the Trinity who was with God in the beginning and through whom all things were made. It is hard to think of God suffering, but that is exactly what happened. In Jesus, God had hands, and we drove spikes through them. In Jesus, God had a voice, and we made it cry out in pain. In Jesus, God wore clothes, and we stripped him naked. In Jesus, God had a heart, and we pierced it with a lance. Begin to prepare now for that tragic Friday when God was forsaken.

> How can this be?
> With accent Galilean
> this upstart Nazarean
> expects us to put stock
> in babbling meant to shock.
> Is this the long awaited
> Messiah we debated?
> Can this be he?

> How can this be?
> This poser from our heartland
> says I AM for a start and
> then pointing up above
> claims rights to special love
> from our Divine Creator.
> The cross will be his fate, or
> can this be He?

Giver of all good things, we took your greatest gift and hung him on a cross because we could not believe how much you would do for love of us. Help us to know in our hearts the full extent of your care and concern for humankind. Let us see you in your Son so that we may grasp the magnitude of your Gift.   Amen.

WEDNESDAY OF THE FIFTH WEEK

Nebuchadnezzar exclaimed, "Blessed be the God of Shadrach, Meshach and Abednego, who sent his angel to deliver the servants that trusted in him; they disobeyed the royal command and yielded their bodies rather than serve or worship any god except their own God."   (Dn 3:95)

Shadrach, Meshach and Abednego would not bow down to a Babylonian idol as commanded by Nebuchadnezzar. They were delivered from the fiery furnace by an angel sent by the God they refused to betray. During Lent we identify those gods we have been bowing down to. They are not the pagan statues we remember from some Cecil B. DeMille extravaganza, not grim-visaged bronze and iron bogeymen. Our idols are more appealing, more user-friendly.

The goddess of youth is certainly a charmer. Bronze only to the depth of her epidermis, this perennial twenty-five year old invites us to be forever young. Her altar is a dressing table covered with ointments, cremes, lotions, hair spray, and wrinkle remover. How much money have we wasted trying to slow the hands of time? That small fortune could have provided some books for the Senior Citizen Center.

The god of ease is a laid-back tour director revealing to us the vast landscape of self-indulgence. There never echoes

Wednesday of the Fifth Week

through his lush valleys the harsh cry of inconvenience. Instead, the brooks are bubbling champagne, the poppies pain killers, while arching over the hills is a rainbow of vacuous entertainments. What have we spent to isolate ourselves from reality? A little of that could have gone a long way at Children's Hospital.

The goddess of power is a seductress bidding us to use our talents to their fullest in recasting the world around us in our own image. Sweet reason is her song. What could be more reasonable than using wit, intelligence, looks, and lineage to propel people along the right way, our way? Ours is the grand design. If others cannot see the wisdom of our plan, we are fully capable of persuading them. To guide each movement of so many puppets requires constant attention. Just a fraction of the energy expended on dominating others could build a community of mutual respect among those with whom we live and work.

All our idols are attractive, but they are base metal. The crucible of self-examination will melt them down, permitting us to form again the image of the God of Shadrach, Meshach and Abednego. This image is the human face of God, One like the Son of Man. Today reform in your heart the image of Jesus Christ, the face of God your world needs to see.

> The atheist who has no God
> is better far than I who call
> myself His faithful son and heir
> while bowing down to gods as small
> as dimes and quarters, base conceits
> about my age, dark strategies
> to win the day for my design,
> and palliatives to grant me ease.

These brazen idols I have formed
bestow on me the vain rewards
I'm sure I cannot live without.
Although I know these loveless lords
gaze back at me with my own eyes
and in my image they are made,
to topple them would wrench my soul
and prove my striving mere charade.

One God and true, move your strong arm
to sweep my pagan altar clear
of all which does not point to you.
I am not asking without fear,
but do now cleanse this pantheon
enclosing my self-serving heart
and free my hands to do your work,
not this poor pagan potter's art.

My only God, forgive me for putting false gods before you. Let my life be remade in your image. May I strive to please you and you alone. Amen.

THURSDAY OF THE FIFTH WEEK

I solemnly assure you, if a man is true to my word he shall never see death. (Jn 8:51)

Television is the source of much that is enlightening, inspiring and noteworthy. Fine arts, sports, educational opportunities, religious insights are ours simply by turning a dial. These uplifting offerings, however, are far outnumbered by the tawdry and debasing dramas and comedies that pass for entertainment in prime time. They make immorality commonplace by repetition and raise our tolerance for disgust at violence. Chief among all the sins of television is this: death is made acceptable.

As the bodies pile up, we keep telling ourselves that it is just fiction, a fantasy not to be identified with real life. But there it is again and again. Two dead in this show, three in the next. The actors seem to accept it; why shouldn't we? Dylan Thomas warned us about going quietly into that dark night. We are going quietly, whole families in front of the screen immune to the gore, deaf to the dying gasp. We have arrived at a distorted fulfillment of Jesus' promise in John's Gospel. Little by little we begin not to see death. It is so pervasive in our media and in our society that it no longer registers.

To Jesus, the greatest evil in the world was death. All sin was a foreshadowing of death. No one could escape death, not even he. The most solemn pronouncements of the prophets were concerned with death and its aftermath. Abraham, Isaac, and Jacob died. When Jesus told the Jews that those faithful to his word would not die, he did not mean that hearts would beat forever but that death would give way to a new kind of living.

The atmosphere of death which our media exhales is a poison gas. It attacks and numbs the healthy fear of death which should be ours. To make death trivial is to make resurrection equally meaningless. There can be no significance in the struggle to preserve life when it is seen to be just another disposable item in our throw-away society.

If you have found yourself becoming more inured to death on the screen, begin today to refresh your appreciation for the last thing that will happen to you. A good start would be a rearrangement of your television viewing. Couple that with a careful reading of the Passion Narratives at the end of each Gospel. Meditate on what really happened to Jesus from the time he left the Garden of Gethsemane to the rending of the Temple veil. His death is your death, not in detail but in effect. Jesus died. So will you and I die. His triumph was not that he avoided death, but that in fighting and losing the battle, he won the war.

> O Death, where is thy sting?
> Not in the weeping
> or in the pain.
> Not in the longing
> to rise again.
> These feelings only spring
> to life in life held tight
> in hope of winning.
> The sting of death
> concludes the dying.
> With one last breath
> a soul has lost the fight.

Giver of life everlasting, I ask not to be rescued from the dying I surely must endure, but from eternal darkness. May your Son's final victory be mine.   Amen.

FRIDAY OF THE FIFTH WEEK

> The breakers of death surged round about me,
>   the destroying floods overwhelmed me;
> The cords of the nether world enmeshed me;
>   the snares of death overtook me.

Friday of the Fifth Week

> In my distress I called upon the Lord
> and cried out to my God;
> From his temple he heard my voice,
> and my cry to him reached his ears. (Ps 18:5-7)

The little boy fairly hopped from his bed and ran to the window. Then his eyes clouded with disappointment. No snow again. He shuffled down the stairs to the kitchen. "I prayed real hard last night," he told his mother as he sat on his Christmas sled, "but I guess his line was busy."

The inspired writer of today's Responsorial Psalm knew that God's line is never busy. It is an open line to all our pleadings, longings, confidences and confessions. God always wants to hear our voices even though the song seldom varies: heal me, forgive me, save me. But he waits in vain for many of us to thank him and praise him for answering our prayers.

Psalm 18 is attributed to David. It is a song of thanksgiving for his deliverance from the hand of Saul. David knew from whence his salvation came, and so do we. There is no doubt in your mind about the source of your happiness. You are certain that God's love was operative in that near-miss on the highway, in the recovery of your lost dog, in that job you finally found. All who call themselves Christians know that God guides each step of their lives. The proof of your reliance upon God's mercy is the time you spend praying to make a bad situation better.

When God does come to our rescue, however, we tend to forget the danger we had been in and what God did for us. Today, when we are so close to God's supreme act of rescue, we should remember to give thanks. The psalmist gives us a simple rule: Give thanks in proportion to the need which was answered. "The breakers of death surged about" David.

"The cords of the nether world enmeshed" him. He praised God for giving his very life back to him.

    Should not you and I do the same? Every morning our lives are given back to us. If that's not enough to move you to give thanks, think of all the close calls that never happened to you yesterday, the very real dangers that never confronted you. A glance at the front page of the newspaper reveals a host of snares which you escaped. Give thanks today that God kept you from harm's way. Praise him for his moment-by-moment deliverance.

> War breaks out near Timbuktu
> Earthquake shatters mountain town
> Hitler murders millionth Jew
> Ferry sinks, a hundred drown
>   Why was I here and not there?
>
> Break-in at the home next door
> Neighbors out of work for weeks
> Hunger plagues the local poor
> House fire caused by gas pipe leaks
>   Why am I held in His care?
>
> Deep depression dogs her still
> Constant pain has made him lame
> Daily drink consumes her will
> He has sullied his good name
>   Why don't I collect my share?
>
> Time will bring the rocky way
> But for now my prayer will be
> Thank you, Lord, for this bright day
> Praise to you for sparing me
>   Why, again I've slipped the snare!

Lord, my rescue and my salvation, accept my praise for your goodness to me. You have kept me from falling into the pit, from dangers never recognized. Thank you for your loving protection. Amen.

SATURDAY OF THE FIFTH WEEK

The chief priests and the Pharisees called a meeting of the Sanhedrin. "What are we to do," they said, "with this man performing all sorts of signs? If we let him go on like this, the whole world will believe in him. Then the Romans will come in and sweep away our sanctuary and our nation." (Jn 11:47-48)

Has the age of miracles passed? The cynics would have us believe that it has. They speak of miracles of faith with disdain while urging us instead to look at the wonders humankind has performed. Today's miracles are seen in our technology, we are told. As Lent draws to a close, take a serious look around you for miracles. Can you see any miracles of faith in your life or in the lives of those close to you?

A young man began to suffer bouts of depression. The attacks grew more frequent until he could barely endure the company of others. Life rubbed him raw. Because everything he heard deepened his feelings of worthlessness, he became a near recluse. He began to see a psychiatrist, first every two weeks, and later twice a week. This counseling brought him brief periods of relief, but his demons always won out.

For nearly two years, the young man struggled against this overpowering self-doubt, barely able to make his way in society. His counselor did not believe in anti-depressant medicine. Finally, the young man moved to a different locale and found a new counselor, a psychiatrist who soon prescribed a drug. Within weeks, the depression lifted; within months, the young man was off the pills and never had to rely on them again. From then on, he was able to control his illness and suffered from blue days about as frequently as you and I do.

Was this a miracle on the level of Jesus' healings in the New Testament? It had all the markings. First, the illness was quite severe. Second, the young man never ceased praying to God for a cure. Third, the depression lifted very rapidly. Fourth, abnormal depression has not burdened this man for seventeen years now. But what about the pills, you say? Didn't they effect the cure? Indeed, they were an important but secondary cause of the healing. It was the young man's faith that God was working through his doctors and, yes, through the inventor of the medicine, that made the miracle possible. This faith opened the young man to God's healing touch. God worked through that faith, the expertise of counselors, and the genius of the inventor to bring good out of something very bad.

This is the essence of any miracle. God uses the things of the world, whether it be the saliva of Jesus or the composition of healing drugs, to bring good out of bad. This was as surely a divine intervention as were the signs which so worried the chief priests and the Pharisees in today's Gospel. Reflect today on those situations in which you have seen God doing his healing work. And don't deny God's healing intervention just because the matter may be minor. What may seem unimportant to you can be to God something of infinite worth.

A wart.
Annoyingly long-lived
a twenty year reproach
resistant to home remedies
so proud one day and gone
the next. What happens to
a wart?

A wart.
Does it demean his might
to claim that God concerns
himself with matters so minute
to reach around a world
in agony and touch
a wart?

Author of miracles, each breath I take, every blade of grass is your victory over death. Help me to recognize and appreciate each promise of resurrection in my daily life so that I may experience fully your essential miracle, Christ's Easter triumph.   Amen.

PASSION SUNDAY

"God save the Son of David! Blessed be he who comes in the name of the Lord! God save him from on high!" (Mt 21:9)

"Crucify him!" they all cried. He said, "Why, what crime has he committed?" But they only shouted the louder, "Crucify him!" (Mt 27:23)

How quickly darkness comes upon the earth when storm clouds sweep across the high prairie. One o'clock in the afternoon of a late July day. The thermometer measures 102 degrees. All things bear the weight of the sun. Even the leaves in the trees are too heavy to move. Then, a faint breeze. Once white, fleecy clouds darken and harden. The breeze becomes a wind with a threatening voice. Shadows race across the sunscape. The prelude is brief. The first drops spatter the dust, lightning flashes, and the ponderous storm machine begins to crawl over the land unleashing the deadly, graygreen fog of electrocuted air. Fury has come to blot out the sun. There is darkness over the whole earth.

"Passion" means "suffering," the Lord's ordeal. But consider also the passions of the crowd. How quickly the emotions of those caught up in the joyous welcome have changed to hate. How many of those who sought to honor him with palm branches later stood jeering as they chose Barabbas? We don't know. That those who threw their cloaks in his path and those who screamed for his crucifixion could be the same people defies logic. Until we look into our own hearts.

The Gospel readings for Passion Sunday compress the action. We enter church today singing hosannas, and in the space of a few minutes, we join our voices in a ritual cry of blood lust. It happens as quickly as a storm sweeps across the plain, as quickly as a sunny day returns to gloom, as quickly as a pure heart turns to evil. We know it happened in Jerusalem as Jesus endured his Passover because we know it has happened again and again in our own hearts darkened by the storm of passions we seem unable to control.

Passion Sunday reminds you and me that no matter how rock-steady our self-control, no matter how blameless our behavior has been, we are vulnerable. Each morning we welcome Jesus into our hearts, laying our hopes and good intentions before him like so many cloaks on the road to Jerusalem. We resolve to make our day a City of God, washed with the warm sun of his love. Then at 10:00 am or Noon or 4:00 pm or 8:00 pm, the storm clouds gather:

irritation, envy, gossip, little things that can lead to great evils. Our passions are aroused, our need for self-approval or self-gratification overpowers our good intentions and the midday darkness is upon us. It happens so fast that we can't believe that we are the same hope-filled persons that greeted the Sun of Justice. How could a hopeful crowd become a hate-filled mob? Look into your own heart.

Today begins Christ's journey to Calvary. We will follow him in his agony and recoil at his vulnerability. In your meditations during this week, do not overlook your own vulnerability. Jesus will endure scourging, spittle, false witness, mockery, and crucifixion because of your vulnerability. More swiftly than the crowd became a mob are you and I overwhelmed by the darkness of evil. We need the strength and trust of Jesus to survive the swift storms of passion that sweep over us. They come without warning; we cannot outmaneuver them. We can only flee. And there is nowhere to run from these sudden storms except to the arms of the Lord.

> Capsuled spacemen mark the sun's rise
> eighteen times a day.
> Dawn and darkness chase each other
> over isle and bay.
>
> Swifter still across my landscape
> race the day and night.
> Moods and passions, coarse alarums
> wound, then slay, the light.
>
> Each new day betrays its promise,
> dusk and death creep in.
> Steadfastness is quickly shadowed
> by the scudding sin.

Burns a beacon with the power
to defeat this gloom?
Yes, the light of resurrection
streams forth from the tomb.

Rise again, O Star of David,
and the night is done.
Make my heart of darkness into
land of midnight sun.

Jesus Christ, my king, come into my heart and reign over my life. May I trust completely in your power and welcome into the depths of my soul the purifying fire of your love. Save me from the darkness of sin and guide me to the Kingdom of Light.   Amen.

MONDAY OF HOLY WEEK

The fact was, the chief priests planned to kill Lazarus too, because many Jews were going over to Jesus and believing in him on account of Lazarus. (Jn 12:10-11)

This is the day to bail out. If you are looking for an opportunity to walk no longer with this Jesus of Nazareth, you will find no better time. The chief priests were after Lazarus because he committed the unpardonable sin of being alive. After four days in the tomb, he came forth to the sound of Jesus' weeping. Now he stands as a reproach to the Jewish leaders who thought they could sweep this Jesus phenomenon under the rug. A person who was dead and now lives cannot be so easily dismissed. Lazarus had to return to the tomb.

On this Monday of Holy Week, John's Gospel confirms

Monday of Holy Week

something we may have only dimly recognized. Not only is it not easy to follow Jesus, it is downright dangerous. The closer you get to Jesus, the more hazardous it becomes. If you are fortunate enough to have been cured by him, you stand in dire peril. If he returned you from death to life you are as good as dead. Here, the Christian paradox is revealed in all its irony.

The closer you get to Jesus, the clearer it is that you don't belong to this world. *In* the world, yes, but not *of* it. Matching his pace step-by-step makes you an outcast, one set apart, a target for the many to whom your way of living is a condemnation of their lifestyles. If you are near enough to be touched by him, healed by him, revived by him, you will reap the harvest of the martyrs.

Today, consider how deeply you are invested in the world. You give in to the world to the degree that you belong to it. That part of you which the world owns cannot belong to Christ. The world will go to great lengths to bind you to itself, to make you a chattel of power or wealth or ease or good standing. When you begin to break the silken strands of slavery to the world, when you start to pull away in order to keep up with Christ's heaven-bound stride, then you and Lazarus begin to march in step; the judgment the chief priests laid upon him falls upon you as well.

Is this the day to cut your losses? Friday looms ever larger on the horizon. If you have spent this season in a serious attempt to let Christ's life shine through you, you are a marked man, a branded woman. The bell has pealed for each day you fasted, for every sacrifice you made, for each good example you provided; it tolls for you. Can you continue to believe in Christ's promises, to seek his healing touch, to live his new life? Four more days and the world will have lost. Do not think it will give up so easily.

The iron stove
glows red with fire
restrains the heat
that I desire.

When I approach
to warm my hands
respect is what
the fire demands.

Too close, my skin
begins to smart.
Too far, the cold
creeps round my heart.

The paradox
is clear to me.
The risk lies in
proximity.

Permit me, Lord,
to come so near
that your warm love
will melt my fear.

Loving Father, let me walk in the footsteps of your Son during these holiest of days. May I never fear the demands of his love or the risks of his sacrifice.   Amen.

TUESDAY OF HOLY WEEK

He (John) leaned back against Jesus' chest and said to him, "Lord, who is he?" Jesus answered, "The one to whom I give the bit of food I dip in the dish." He dipped the morsel, then took it and gave it to Judas, son of Simon Iscariot. Immediately after, Satan entered his heart. Jesus addressed himself to him, "Be quick about what you are to do." (Jn 13:25-27)

We all know betrayal. A child tells on his playmate. A woman gossips about her friend. An executive climbs the corporate ladder over the broken careers of those he has stabbed in the back. Who among us would be so naive as to give a gift to our betrayer?

Jesus did exactly that in today's Gospel. Even now in the Middle East, a host at dinner will honor a guest by personally preparing an especially succulent portion of food and serving it to him. Jesus dipped a morsel in the dish and gave it to Judas to show him that it was not too late, that the process of betrayal could be stopped even at the eleventh hour. Aware that Judas' plan was already in motion, the Master sought to dissuade him. With the honor of offering him the host's special gift went Jesus' unspoken pledge of trust in Judas' better instincts. He was telling him that it could all end here rather than with a traitor's kiss at the edge of the Garden.

As you meditate today on the part you play in the daily betrayal of Jesus, remember that it can all stop here. It is not necessary to give in to the temptation; you are not foreordained to take the next evil step; the inertia of sin is not absolute.

How to stop it? How stay your hand from betrayal? Think of this scene from John's Gospel and the words that Judas could have said: "Master, I want to turn away from my set path. Give me the strength to step back from the brink." You know he will honor your request as surely as he honored Judas with the host's beneficence.

Since we are certain that Jesus will give us the power to overcome any temptation, the difficulty lies in making the request. There's the rub. The strength to resist is ours for the asking. We don't ask because we want the evil result. In the face of our determination to complete the dreadful act, Jesus is powerless. We have made him so by refusing to make the one request which could turn us around. Today, consider your habits of sin. In each instance, you will find that moment when you stood on the brink, when it was within your power to employ the strength that Jesus offered. Resolve to make better use of that decisive moment.

The turning point
  lies dead
    ahead
	the urges which
	  betray
	    His way

a moment's pause
  to make
    or break
	His strength awaits
	  your best
	    request

Each act affords
  an inch
    to flinch
	Unless you ask
	  the sin
	    will win

a time to ask
  can grace
    replace
	The choice is clear
	  to call
	    or fall

All-powerful God, keep me from the evil which attracts me so. At the moment of temptation, I will call out to you and you will answer. Show me your path and give me the strength to follow it.   Amen.

WEDNESDAY OF HOLY WEEK

In the course of the meal he said, "I give you my word, one of you is about to betray me." Distressed at this, they began to say to him one after another, "Surely it is not I, Lord?" (Mt 26:21-22)

Wednesday of Holy Week

Today, we are given a glimpse into the minds of Jesus' closest companions. Each of them appears to have grounds for believing that Jesus could rightly accuse him of betrayal. "Surely it is not I, Lord?" might better be written "Surely you have not found me out, Lord?" An avowal of innocence does not end with a question mark.

With the exception of the heinous plan of Judas, the acts for which the Apostles are ashamed were probably minor treacheries: failure to be as kind to the poor as Jesus was; taking some time out to return to commercial fishing as insurance against the day when the Master was found out to be a false Messiah; resentment over the favored place of Peter, James and John; falling asleep during the twentieth repetition of the Sermon on the Mount.

Tomorrow begins the Sacred Triduum, three days of earth-shaking evil on the part of the Jewish authorities, three days of minor treacheries on the part of the Eleven. For the most part, the Gospels spare us a detailed account of the frailties of those closest to Jesus. The blanks are easy to fill in, however. If we want to see the weaknesses of his friends, we need only to look at our own lives.

As you stand on the threshold of these three days that shook the world, consider the minor treacheries that surrounded Judas' great betrayal: the flight of fair-weather friends; Peter's fear of guilt by association; Pilate's unwillingness to get involved; soldiers just following orders. Can you not see these same sad events played out in your world, perhaps in your own life? You may have turned your back on a friend who espoused an unpopular view. Or perhaps you kept silent about an injustice because you knew you would have to make a sacrifice to right it. Has an overzealous dedication to duty kept you from being compassionate? These are the "little sins" that began to snowball during the first Holy Week. They ended in a tragedy of cosmic proportions.

As you follow Jesus through these last days, make his path your examination of conscience. Pay particular attention to all those seemingly insignificant decisions made by the supporting actors in this melancholy drama. A contrary choice, a pause to reflect, a "no" to self-centeredness may have altered, not the outcome, of course, but the plot. It won't be difficult to see yourself in this play; each of us commits the same little murders every day.

Peter James John	dozed
Annas Caiaphas	plotted
Sanhedrin	connived
Herod	feared
Peter	denied
Witnesses	lied
Crowd	shouted
Pilate	demurred
Guards	mocked
Onlookers	jeered
Simon of Cyrene	balked
Ten	fled
Soldiers	gambled
Thieves	scorned
I	concurred

Father of mercy, You know my little betrayals. By themselves they don't amount to much. Taken together they pave the road to Calvary. Let me see the full effect of my sins so that I may renounce the evil done and resolve to do no more. Amen.

HOLY THURSDAY

> Thus he came to Simon Peter, who said to him, "Lord, are you going to wash my feet?" Jesus answered, "You may not realize now what I am doing, but later you will understand." Peter replied, "You shall never wash my feet!" "If I do not wash you," Jesus answered, "you will have no share in my heritage." (Jn 13:6-8)

Some years ago, a popular book called *The Peter Principle* was based on the premise that too often a person climbing the managerial ladder was promoted one step above his capacity to manage. A Christian variation on this theme could be called "The Simon Peter Principle," a rule which holds that St. Peter, the Apostle, was always over his head when assaying the humanity of Jesus. From the day Jesus called Peter "Satan" for supposing that he could escape human suffering to the night before he died, Peter clung to the belief that Jesus was somehow too good or too holy or too powerful to have to submit to the evil designs of his persecutors. To Peter's mind, it was impossible that the Master could be so humbled.

The "Simon Peter Principle" lives on today in all of us who think that Jesus merely donned a cloak of humanity and went through the motions of human trial and suffering to set an example for the rest of us who are mired in the flesh. We pin our hopes on a God who could throw off his mantle of flesh at any moment and strike dead his tormentors. When alone in intimacy with this savior, we say with Peter, "You shall never wash my feet," meaning, "Come on, I know who you really are. You can drop your pose with me."

In the Gospel for Holy Thursday, Jesus makes our acceptance of his total and authentic humanity a requirement for sharing in his heritage. To be Christian means much more than believing in God's Son come to earth. It means accepting the fact that God could be, and chose to be, and was humiliated ... not just humble, but humiliated. We have seen kings and presidents and Popes behave humbly. We know they can drop the pose any time. But Jesus couldn't drop the pose. It was no pose. Once he made the choice to drain the cup of suffering, there was no turning back. In the Upper Room when he bent to the basin, in Gethsemane when he accepted his Father's will, on the cross when he refused the drugged wine, Jesus was not just behaving like a human being. He was accepting once again, as he did all his life, the humiliation of suffering, the humiliation of being powerless, the humiliation of being human. He did it not as a grand gesture of condescension toward his subjects or as a regal example of piety. He bent to the basin because a fully human being could find no other way of expressing infinite love.

John's Gospel makes no explicit mention of the institution of the Eucharist in the Upper Room. Scholars ponder the reason for this omission and conclude that John accepted the depictions of the other Evangelists as sufficient. Perhaps the Fourth Evangelist, whose work is called the Gospel of Glory, sought to forestall any misinterpretation of his portrayal of the power and authority of Christ. Now, on the last night of his life, Jesus bends to the basin and brings us back to earth again, back to the world of suffering humanity where for so many people every day brings with it the humiliation of being weak, broken, human.

Tonight, before you receive Holy Communion, the sign of the Divine Banquet, you will see one of your brothers bend to the basin at the feet of twelve wounded people. Bend down with him, bend low with him and the Master, bend to the basin in thanksgiving that your flesh and their flesh and His flesh are one flesh.

Holy Thursday

Unlikely gift, this Eucharist,
a simple supper, common fare
compels Omnipotence to bend
to earth and save a sinner there.

Where is the mighty tread of God,
Colossus striding forth to shake
the very pillars of the earth
and cause all sullied hearts to quake?

Outside an upper room at dusk
a mockingbird adds evensong
to homesick hymns of Galilee
from voices straining to be strong.

No shafts of Zeus to split the air
and make the cedars writhe in flame.
No Caesar marshalling his hosts
to make the nations praise his name.

A man who shares a humble meal
with friends afraid of morning's sun,
in benediction wipes their feet:
Bend to the bowl as I have done.

Lord of Life, you humbled yourself so that we might see ourselves in you. In you we see our high destiny. In you we see our model of service to our brothers and sisters. As you fed your followers with your Body and Blood, so let us nourish the needy of our world with the gift of self. Amen.

GOOD FRIDAY

The soldiers came and broke the legs of the men crucified with Jesus, first of the one, then of the other. When they came to Jesus and saw that he was already dead, they did not break his legs. One of the soldiers thrust a lance into his side, and immediately blood and water flowed out. (Jn 19:32-24)

SOP. The Roman Army had Standard Operating Procedures for every duty, including crucifixion. The condemned man would first be scourged as a sign of his abasement. Then his arms would be stretched out and tied to a single crosspiece which he would have to bear to the place of execution. Our liturgical art mistakenly pictures Jesus carrying the completed cross on one shoulder. But Roman SOP required the upright section of the cross to be permanently implanted in the ground. When the condemned man reached the site of his death, he would be hoisted to the top of the upright pole. His arms remained tied to the crosspiece or, in the case of Jesus, nails would be driven through his wrists.

Men would live for many hours, sometimes days, suspended from the cross. They would agonizingly push themselves up and down on the cross, staving off asphyxiation by stretching and bending their legs to force air into and out of their lungs. Sometimes, outside circumstances, such as a religious law prohibiting burials on the Sabbath, would cause the guards to hasten death by breaking the legs of the crucified, thus putting an end to his tortured breathing.

Sabbath began at nightfall, so the Jewish leaders asked Pilate to have the legs broken of the three men who hung on Calvary. The guards performed this grisly mercy for the two thieves, but found that Jesus was already dead. He lived but three hours on the cross when others had lived for days.

Good Friday

Jesus died relatively quickly because of the weight he bore to Calvary. Not the weight of the crosspiece, a rough log six feet long weighing thirty to forty pounds. Added to that was the weight of the sins of mankind. It is impossible for us to understand the meaning of a statement like, "He took upon himself the guilt of us all." It means literally that Jesus was guilty of every sin ever committed. We shy away from connecting the Sinless One with even a hint of iniquity. Yet, we can reach no other conclusion. The horrible irony is that, although he committed not one of them, Jesus accepted the guilt for each and every sin that men and women have committed and will commit. This is the burden he carried to Calvary. This is the weight that crushed his soul. This is the guilt that broke his heart.

Good Friday is a day to feel guilty, to feel the weight of your sins as they push down upon your soul. There is no greater burden than guilt. It crushes hope, distorts perspective, flattens the spirit. We would not have the strength to contemplate our guilt every day, but for one day we should try to experience at least part of what Jesus endured on the way to Calvary. We can bear mockery, spittle, scourging, even a crown of thorns, but we cannot long bear our guilt, a small part of the burden that crushed the life out of Jesus.

Dwelling on one's guilt is not SOP for the hopeful Christian, but today we must try to feel what Jesus felt. The One who never sinned was crushed by my sins and yours. On this dark Friday, take up his burden and stagger under the load.

> Heat waves rise from baking stones
>   of city walls undulating
>   to the beat of a crowd's catcalls.
>   Are these the walls that wailed?

Blood and sweat in my eyes
   give bystanders the rosy glow
      of too much wine at festival time.
         Are these my people who bleed?

Constellations in broad daylight
   whirl before me planets of pain
      exploding in my shriveling sky.
         Are these Ezekiel's wheels?

A woman in her silence stands apart
   looking through me knowing all now
      keening in the dust for her Jesse.
         Are these her last lullabies?

Up the hill march ribs jaws skulls
   sun-bleached blotted red from my feet
      drinking from an empty font.
         Are these the bones that dance?

Iron invites flesh to part
   and receive an artisan's measured thrusts
      between what's left of me and me.
         Are these the pinions of guilt?

Snatches of verse from prayerful memory
   lift me higher than the soldiers planned
      as eagles contend with carrion crows.
         Are these the evening stars?

The rueful look up to me now past me
   to the sudden black of my mantle
      my Father's cloak about the city's shoulders.
         Are these my brothers and sisters?

All-merciful Father, you allowed this man, our brother, your only-begotten Son, to be crushed by my guilt. He chose the path of death so that he might encounter me there and show me a better way. As I acknowledge my parth in his agony, let me follow more closely in his footsteps. They are easy to find they are marked with the blood he spilled for me. Amen.

HOLY SATURDAY

> The hand of the Lord came upon me, and he led me out in the spirit of the Lord and set me in the center of the plain, which was now filled with bones. He made me walk among them in every direction so that I saw how many they were on the surface of the plain. How dry they were! He asked me: "Son of man, can these bones come to life?" "Lord God," I answered, "you alone know that." (Ez 37:1-3)

It is unusually quiet in Jerusalem, even for a Sabbath. Yesterday's incredible events have stunned the populace. There have been crucifixions before. Others calling themselves saviors of the people have mounted the Hill of the Skull. Brave men and cowards have hung on other crosses, but none have brought down upon the city an eclipse of the sun. None called forth the bodies of the dead. The curtain in the Temple always remained intact.

Jerusalem is quiet with relief, a mother's relief that the agony of childbirth is over. Another stillborn messiah has been laid in his grave. It is no accident that his mourners are hard to find. Some have fled the city. Others weep on borrowed pillows. Some recall in hushed tones his miracles, his healings, his preaching. "He did... He was... He said..."

Jesus of Nazareth has become past tense. Today, perhaps, gone but not forgotten. Tomorrow, forgotten.

There is something unusual about your local church on this Saturday. It is not just empty; it is bare, lacking any vestige of ceremony. The golden doors of the tabernacle swing wide offering a glimpse of useless splendor. There is nothing so empty as an empty tabernacle. The altar stands stripped, embarrassed to admit what all can see: it is just a table. Abandoned by its family, it has no function. Its magnetic attraction for people, its mysterious power to gather the disparate elements of the community has been switched off by the hand of calamity. Your church this day is a little Jerusalem, bereft of life, echoing with yesterday's jeers and supplications.

Except for one thing. The difference between your church on this Saturday and Jerusalem on that long ago Sabbath is the factor of anticipation. There was no anticipation in Jerusalem. No one was waiting. The man was dead. Like the thieves who died with him, like all the messiahs who preceded him, he rested now in Sheol, that dim chamber from which no one has ever returned. The play had closed. None of the actors — mother, friends, followers, betrayer, soldiers, priests — would ever mount this stage again. The Hero was dead. The curtain is down.

The quiet of your church, however, is that of *entr'acte*. The faithful will soon return bearing new scenery and costumes. In the community, the anticipation is palpable. Men and women are waiting for the next act. They have been reading the Script for two thousand years. Agony and betrayal were prelude. This dark Saturday is but one scene in a continuing drama of light.

Spend this day waiting. If just waiting seems not enough for you, think of that Sabbath in Jerusalem when there was nothing to wait for. Think of that city burying its past in

Holy Saturday

mournful memory, the bereaved taking their leave of the Master. Then, there was no hope.

Now, we live in hope. "Son of man, can these bones come to life?" "Lord God, you alone know that." We live in the hope that the Lord God's answer will be no different from that welcomed by Noah, Abraham, Joseph, Moses, Ezekiel and Mary. The answer is a promise heavy with new life. The promise is a Word that takes on flesh. The Word is a Weaver who knits together bones with threads of sinew and muscle. The Weaver sings his worksong: "Wait, children of Israel. People of God, wait."

>Dry, dry the bones of our fathers.

>Long since has living flesh encased
>the alabaster skeletons.
>The inner force that once held fast
>a matrix of a million suns,
>a galaxy of thought and act,
>has melted in the desert sand,
>pulled down to miry netherworld,
>there rudely cupped in Death's dark hand.

>Dry, dry the bones of our fathers.

>Once rang the littered valley green
>with cries of children at their play.
>Of light and life the wise man spoke
>assuring all that each new day
>is but a promise of the next.
>He did not see, they did not know
>life's orbit swung erratically
>attracted by a world below.

Dry, dry the bones of our fathers.

Quite powerless are those who seed
a universe with stars that think
when deep beneath this hapless vale
the magnet Death decides to drink.
Flesh falls from flesh and bone from bone.
We lie with generations past
awaiting One who conquers Death.
The Son of Man will come at last.

Dry, dry the bones of our fathers.

Father of the heavens and the earth, as we await the outcome of the titanic struggle of these three days, give us the gift of hope. We can do nothing but trust in your mercy and compassion for the powerless. We rely solely on the might of your hand and the obedience of your Son, Jesus Christ, our Lord.   Amen.

EASTER SUNDAY

Suddenly, without warning, Jesus stood before them and said, "Peace!" The women came up and embraced his feet and did him homage. At this Jesus said to them. "Do not be afraid! Go and carry the news to my brothers that they are to go to Galilee, where they will see me." (Mt 28:9-10)

A fearsome thing, this new world. Again and again it is necessary for Jesus to reassure his disciples: "Do not be afraid. Peace. Do not be frightened. Peace be with you." This was not at all what they had expected. They had expected nothing new. The women came with oils to anoint the body — not a pleasant task, but a necessary, time-

Easter Sunday

honored ritual of respect for the dead and obedience to the Law. They had loved the Master and would perform for him this final act of mercy.

Approaching the tomb, they stepped into a new creation, a world of figures in dazzling white and guards lying paralyzed on the ground. Although Jesus had made many attempts to prepare his followers for these wonders, the habits of death are hard to break. Anoint the cold flesh. Wrap the stiffening body. Seal the dank tomb. Anoint, wrap, seal: the way of a world governed by death. Who, in her most fantastic imaginings, would suspect that the path to this tomb led to a second Genesis?

In three days, God had remade the world in the image of his Son. From the chaos of Good Friday emerged the new Adam, the Easter Man. For the exiles of Eden, the way east was illuminated by the fiery sword of the angel guarding the Tree of Life. Now an angel in dazzling white pointed the way to the new Eden. The disobedience of Adam and Eve made them subject to death. The obedience of Jesus made him firstborn of the new creation, a resurrected world to be peopled by a race that could live forever. No wonder Jesus had to counter the women's fear. The very air was electric with a new kind of life: oxygen, nitrogen, and immortality.

Two thousand years later, we are the sophisticated heirs of those frightened women. Twenty centuries of tradition, a childhood of catechisms, a lifetime of sermons have had their effect. And that effect is too often a routine of creeds and liturgies that lull us into taking for granted the act of the world's re-creation which is the core of our faith. We are not amazed anymore.

Easter Sunday is a day to examine our capacity for amazement, to take seriously the role so admirably filled by the eyewitnesses to the Resurrection. In an age when prodigies and calamities gush from our living room screens, it is not easy to be amazed. Very little surprises us after we've seen the mushroom cloud over Hiroshima and the ovens at Auschwitz and the skeletons of Ethiopia. Death has thickened our skins. And in taking death for granted, we begin to take life for granted. We fiddle in the womb with test tubes and cultures. We decide who has a right to life and who has a duty to die.

Easter challenges us to rediscover our fear of death and our awe of life. In the early 18th century, Isaac Watts captured the melancholy inevitability of death in these lines from "O God, Our Help in Ages Past":

> Time, like an ever-rolling stream,
> Bears all its sons away;
> They fly forgotten, as a dream
> Dies at the opening day.

What we, who take Easter seriously, celebrate this day is the fact that the ever-rolling stream need not flow unchecked. With the women at the tomb, we stand amazed at a Power greater than death dwelling among us. No one caught in the flood tide of time can be complacent in the face of Christ's triumph. In the depths of our souls, the fear of death gives way to the bright promise of tomorrow. This is tomorrow. Christian, be ye amazed.

Easter Sunday

A whisper in the wind
invites the chirping bird
to pause and cock her head
to question what she heard:
He lives.

The muffled thunder speaks
to cattle in the fields
beneath a cloudless sky.
The message is revealed:
He lives.

A tremor in the earth
too slight to make its mark
except upon those souls
that languish in the dark:
He lives.

In this frenetic world
few take the time to hear
the wondrous words of life
that thwart the ancient fear:
He lives.

The raucous blare of self,
the rumble of machines
combine to dull the mind
to what this Easter means:
He lives.

But soft beneath the din
repeats the ancient cry,
a murmur in the heart
that wishes not to die:
He lives.

O Christian, bow your head
to hear that inner voice
that speaks of death and life
and offers you the choice:
He lives.

God's trumpet you must be
to this unheeding race.
Newborn your deathless song,
two notes of saving grace:
He lives!

Lord of everlasting life, help us to go forth and tell the Good News to our brothers and sisters. May our every word and action proclaim the glory of your resurrection. As sons and daughters of the New Creation, let us amaze the world with your bright promise of immortality. Amen.

A FINAL WORD

The days of Easter are bathed in the radiance of the Lord's resurrection. As the warm spring sun beckons the flowers to burst from the bud, so the glory of the Risen Christ calls us to step forward into a new life. The time of preparation is over. What we have longed for has come to pass.

If only this season of grace could last forever. If only spring were eternal. The sun will keep shining, but clouds will hide its light. the Lord of life will reign forever, but old habits will creep back to obscure our vision of his victory. How does the Christian hold back the shadows which he or she fought so hard to eliminate during the last six weeks? By employing the same methods of purification and penance after Easter as before. Besides being a season of preparation, Lent was also a season of practice, a time of training in which we learned how to preserve our new, deeper relationships with God and neighbor. Lent wasn't simply a prologue to one great day of glory, but a school for holiness in which we experienced a better way to live.

Use the lessons of Lent when the shadow of sin threatens your vision of the Risen Christ. The hard-won victories of the Serious Season cost you too much to be discarded on Easter Sunday. Your new intimacy with God, your revived concern for your brothers and sisters are too precious to be put away until next year. Don't make the mistake I made when I was a little boy. I was taught not only to give up things for Lent but also to make positive resolutions, such as being extra-nice to my playmates. In my childish way, I looked forward to Easter when I wouldn't have to be so nice anymore. Don't be a little boy or a little girl when it comes to extending the blessings of the Serious Season beyond Easter. You have achieved a deepening of prayer life, of concern for neighbor, of sacramental involvement. This deepening has tapped your spiritual depths and brought about a new wholeness of your life in the Lord. But this re-integration of the spirit is still a delicate flower. It must be tended if it is to continue to bloom. God has given you the tools. You've learned how to use them. Resolve to keep your garden growing.

May the lessons of these forty days keep you close to Christ and the children of the Resurrection. May you be whole and holy in his Spirit. May our heavenly Father watch over you and keep you close.